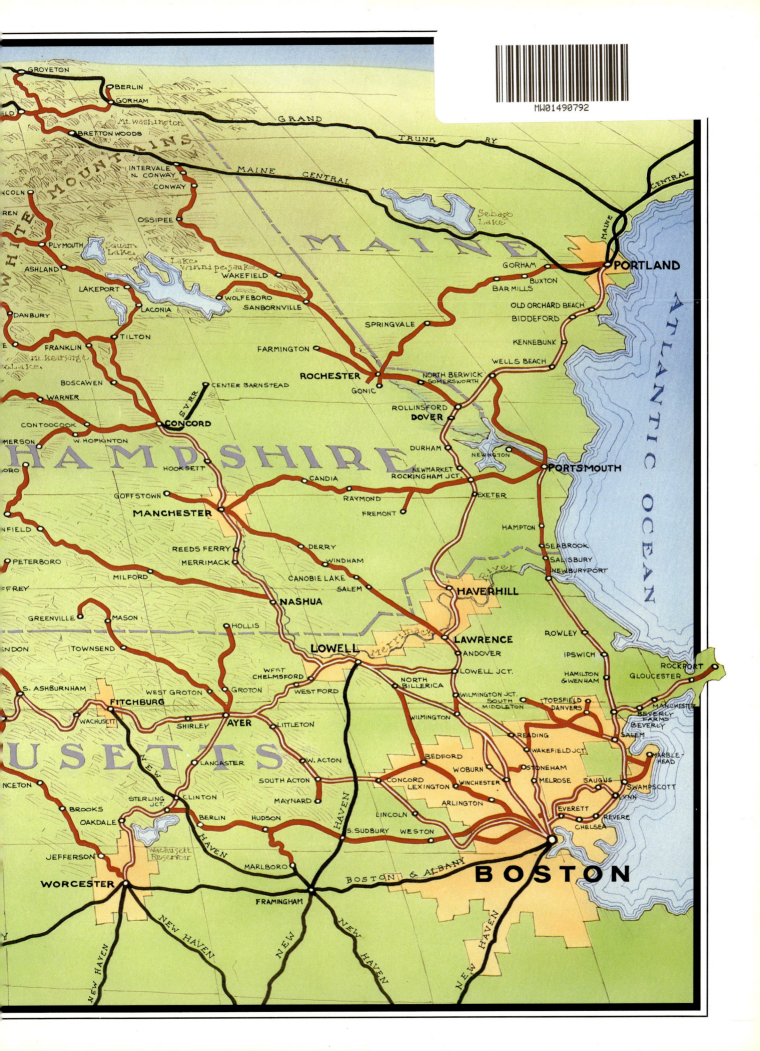

BOSTON & MAINE

Three Colorful Decades
Of New England Railroading

Boston and Maine

Three Colorful Decades
Of New England Railroading

by Robert Willoughby Jones

Pine Tree Press - Los Angeles, California

FRONT COVER: On a beautiful, sunny May 30, 1954, Norton D. Clark and three army buddies visited the mouth of the Hoosac Tunnel, where they photographed a westbound freight with an A-B-B-A set of FTs headed by 4213. Note the multi-bulbed headlight.

REAR COVER ABOVE: The front half of this vintage steam train has crossed the Forest River Bridge into Salem from Marblehead, deadheading commuter coaches to Salem for the night. Neighborhood children are swimming on this beautiful June 3, 1952 afternoon, the brakeman is about to step down to flag the Lafayette Street crossing, and all's right with the world.

REAR COVER BELOW: Four pristine GP-9s in the McGinnis "Bluebird" scheme haul a train across the Deerfield River on an overcast fall day in 1970. Stephen B. Horsley photo.

FRONTISPIECE: The ball signal—surely a unique symbol of New England railroading—shown here at the Boston & Maine-Maine Central junction at Whitefield, New Hampshire in 1951. Sunday-only train No. 6056, in the care of Pacific 3668, heads south to Woodsville for connections to both Boston and New York. Of 16 ball signals operating during the 1940s, only this one at Whitefield survived into the 1980s. Donald Robinson photo.

FRONT ENDSHEET: A system map of the Boston & Maine as it existed circa 1947. A single red line indicates single track; a double red line indicates double track. Black lines indicate other railroads; many (but not all) connecting lines are shown. John Signor is the artist.

REAR ENDSHEET: Through the generosity of Malcolm Woronoff of Aerial Photos International, Inc. of Boston, we are able to provide this aerial view of North Station taken June 22, 1936, amply illustrating the scope of the physical plant just prior to the period covered by this book.

BOSTON & MAINE—Three Colorful Decades of New England Railroading

Edited by Paul Hammond and David Giglio

Layout and design by Katie Kern • Maps by John Signor

Chapter head illustrations by Pamela Jones Aamodt

Color separations by Quadcolor, Burbank, California

Printing and Binding by Walsworth Publishing Company, Marceline, Missouri

Manufactured in the United States of America

Second Printing: Winter 1998

ISBN 0-9640356-4-2 (previously ISBN 0-87046-101-X)
Published by Pine Tree Press, P. O. Box 39484, Los Angeles, California 90039
Originally published in 1991 by Interurban Press, Glendale, California

Library of Congress Cataloging-in-Publication Data

Jones, Robert Willoughby, 1946-
     Boston & Maine—Three Colorful Decades of New England Railroading
     / by Robert Willoughby Jones; foreword by George Drury.
     p.   cm.
     Includes bibliographical references and index.
     ISBN 0-87046-101-X
     1. Boston and Maine Railroad.   I.   Title
    TF25 .B8J66 1991
    385' . 0974—dc20   91-2112
                                                                   CIP

Who in the world would want a picture of a train?

Spoken by a woman to the author as he photographed trains at Swampscott, July 1990.

In a scene to warm the hearts of steam fans everywhere, B&M Pacific 3667 has come to the rescue and is towing a disabled FT-A & B to Boston through Winchester in June 1954. T. J. Donahue photo.

TABLE OF CONTENTS

A very, very cold December 30, 1966, and the car knocker at Mechanicville, New York is burning cotton waste to unfreeze the brake shoe rigging on GP-18 1753. John F. Kane photo.

FOREWORD

By George Drury

The first railroad we encounter colors our subsequent encounters with others. Robert Jones and I share that first railroad, the Boston & Maine. I have six years on him, so I saw a mostly-steam railroad; he saw one nearly dieselized. He saw a different part of the railroad, a secondary line (he'd dispute that adjective, but I mean secondary in the railroad's view, not in his view). By way of compensation, his part of the B&M had a rich network of branch lines; my experience was solely mainline.

My early contacts with the Boston & Maine were, of course, guided by adults. A neighbor took me to the station in Reading, Massachusetts, to watch the *Flying Yankee,* that Down-East *Zephyr* look-alike. I was four, if that, and was already fascinated by trains, but it is a wonder that my fascination survived the sudden burst of noise and stainless steel and dust fifteen feet away.

About the same time we went to Chicago to visit my maternal grandparents. We rode the *Minute Man,* probably to avoid having to change stations in Boston rather than to make sure I could color the line in my map years later. My mother pointed out the electric engines that pulled us through the Hoosac Tunnel, and I remember seeing a brightly painted locomotive nearby. It must have been one of B&M's FTs. The Pullman sleeping car was the only piece of the *Minute Man* that went beyond Troy, New York, and the B&M must have delivered it to the New York Central late, because Mother discovered, when she went in search of a nightcap somewhere west of Albany, that the car was tacked to the rear of a mail train instead of the *Lake Shore Limited.* She didn't reject the B&M because of that; she rode it to Boston regularly for shopping. She didn't ride it often enough to remember that the "K" footnote in the timetable meant Saturday only. She'd have a leisurely lunch, then take the subway back to North Station in anticipation that the k1:25 would get her back to Reading before we got home from school. The 2:30 train just about did.

Dad, on the other hand, never rode the B&M after four years of commuting from Lowell to Boston during his university years, but he encouraged my hobby. We had a grade crossing and overpass ritual. We looked, and if we spied a train approaching in the distance, we waited to watch it go by. Usually, though, it was (look left)

"Nope," (look right) "Nope." The Sunday morning routine was unchanging: stop at Charles's to get the *Boston Herald* and the *New York Times,* get $2 worth of gas (a week's supply) at the Esso station, wait for a Portland-bound train with a pair of E-7s up front and stainless steel coaches in the consist to stop at the station; then go to Sunday school.

Then I discovered the B&M on my own. The bicycle was the emancipator. I could ride to the station and watch trains, using the times in the Reading-Boston pocket timetable as a guide. Trains that went through without stopping were bonuses, and the ticket agent willingly answered my questions about them. One summer noon a friend and I pedaled to the station to see the *Flying Yankee,* due to zip through at 12:16. I was disappointed that it was just a maroon diesel and stainless steel cars, not the Budd-built streamliner.

My first encounters with other railroads were in print. At the public library I quickly exhausted the railroad resources of the children's room. The librarians graciously gave me access to the adult room, which had a file of *TRAINS* Magazine plus a collection of books that was mostly Lucius Beebe (though a local boy, he never gave the B&M enough attention in his books, I thought) and S. Kip Farrington plus Archie Robertson's *Mixed Train Daily* and Frederick Richardson and Nelson Blount's *Along the Iron Trail.* They were enough to broaden my knowledge of railroads, and by the time I was in junior high school I could identify all but one or two photos in the AAR set of prints—you remember those, with all the names painted over and "North and South Railroad" carefully lettered in.

The library introduced me in an odd way to the Canadian Pacific. In *Dahl's Boston,* a collection of cartoons by Francis W. Dahl, editorial cartoonist of the *Boston Herald,* and commentary by Charles W. Morton (Little, Brown and Company, Boston, 1946), I came across this description of the B&M:

North Station is something else again, used by the Boston & Maine and apparently by some Canadian Road, whose red cars have a disconcerting way of popping up in the middle of a train of honest B&M coaches. North Station has nothing to do with any other stations and it is nowhere

The famous 6000, which began its long life in 1935 as the Flying Yankee, *is leaving North Station in the mid 1950s as the* Minute Man. *Passengers on this 4:00 p.m. departure could avail themselves of a buffet during the four hour, ten minute run to Troy, New York.*

During its long service life, it also ran as the Cheshire, *the* Mountaineer, *and the* Businessman. *This is a fine view of North Station before construction of the Expressway which would eventually drain away business so badly. Arthur E. Mitchell photo.*

near them either. I believe the B&M has electric lights on most of its trains but it has been loathe to trade in its wooden cars for the flashier "vestibule" steel coaches that came in around 1903. The B&M could best be described by explaining that its crack summer commuting train, known as the "Millionaires' Special," has retained its original green plush, open platforms, and wooden construction and that it takes fifty-five minutes to cover the thirty-two miles from Boston to Gloucester. The "millionaires" are perhaps putative, but the train does carry one man who is met by a chauffeur at Manchester;* it also carries anyone else who owns or rents a summer residence east of Beverly.

The B&M claims to have a train that goes all the way to Chicago—The *Minute Man*—but I have never met anyone who has tried it out. On information and belief, I can only say the *Minute Man* goes to Troy, N.Y., shifts its Chicago cars to a train to Albany, where they are hooked onto the remnants of still another train, which left Boston's South Station after the *Minute Man's* departure from North Station.

*Some commuters doubt that this man really 'has money'—too expensively dressed, they say.

I was mystified. Why would red Canadian Pacific coaches stand out in a train of red B&M cars? It was 20 years before I learned that the B&M switched from green paint to red on its passenger cars about the time the book was published.

As I read, I unconsciously divided the world of railroading: "We have those too" and "I've never see any of those." I kept an informal mental list of things I saw and therefore believed. Pacifics and Consolidations, naturally, and the range of wood, steel, and stainless steel passenger cars. I saw my first Mogul on the New Hampshire Division in Wilmington (Dad liked the ice cream at a dairy there) and also my first open-platform observation car, on the rear of the *Alouette* from Montreal—and a Canadian Pacific E-8 was pulling the train.

I measured other roads against the B&M. A Ten-Wheeler on a Denver & Salt Lake passenger train? B&M used Pacifics. Only two cars? Five or six was the usual minimum in Reading. Single track? B&M, at least my corner of it, was double track.

Gas-electric cars? Nothing like that showed up in Reading. They were the sort of thing roads like the Burlington and the Union Pacific had, out in the terra incognita west of the Hudson. Then one Saturday morning east of Manchester, New Hampshire, the grade-crossing ritual paid off. As we crossed the tracks, I looked west and saw a headlight. Dad obligingly pulled the car over, and my eyes widened as a real live genuine gas-electric gurgled past toward Portsmouth. More than that, it was pulling another exotic item, a mail-coach trailer.

Mixed trains? Where I lived, B&M had enough passengers to fill passenger trains every hour or so. Considering how long the local freight took to do its work in Reading, I could imagine just how slow a trip on a mixed train might be. Later, careful reading of the system timetable turned up only one mixed train, on the Ashuelot Branch out of Keene, N. H. A few years after that, I saw one in the flesh at Epping, on the same Concord & Portsmouth line that had shown me my first gas-electric: a GP-7, a few freight cars, and a wood combine on which I noticed curved caboose-type handrails.

Articulateds? B&M had none that I knew of. (Much later I learned there were four 2-6-6-2s flogged off to Maine Central after a few years, and two 0-8-8-0s for hump service at Mechanicville.) I compared the Super Chief's run of 2,227 miles with the 12 miles from Reading to Boston—shoot, it was more than B&M's entire route mileage.

Eventually I saw other railroads in person. A day trip to New York in 1957 provided what is now known as a quantum leap. The train sped along for a whole hour at a time between stops, and as it crossed the Thames River at New London, Connecticut, I saw that steam was still alive on the Central Vermont. West of New Haven the line was four tracks and electrified. It may have been the first time I admitted to myself that the Boston & Maine was not a top-rank railroad.

I went to college in Maine but saw little of the Maine Central. Only one passenger train went through Lewiston during daylight hours, and there was plenty on campus to keep me busy. Graduate school in Delaware introduced me to the Pennsylvania Railroad (four tracks and electrified) and the Baltimore & Ohio.

The B&O, as I think back, had something in common with the Boston & Maine (in addition to the 4-8-2s it purchased from the B&M in 1947). It, too, was not a top-rank railroad, and it had more than its share of enthusiasts. It is one of a small group of railroads that railfans choose as their second railroad ("My favorite railroad is . . . but I also like . . . "). I think some railroads have only regional appeal. To my mind, you'd have to grow up near the Louisville & Nashville or the Western Pacific or maybe even the New York Central to choose it as your primary railroad. Some railroads require a total enthusiasm that leaves no room for any other. I can't imagine a Santa Fe fan saying, "But I also

It's the weekend, and a commuter train awaits the Monday morning rush in the quiet company of the turntable and water tower at Reading, Massachusetts. Russell F. Munroe photo.

Sometimes the confluence of railroad equipment, interesting scenery and great weather are especially breathtaking, as they are here on this breezy 1954 afternoon at Wakefield Junction, Massachusetts. The engineer of southbound GP-7 1572 waves to his counterpart on a northbound commuter. T. J. Donahue photo.

like . . . "Or Pennsy or Great Northern (maybe its the Belpaire fireboxes). The Colorado narrow gauge lines go beyond that—they are a cult. A few railroads gather more than regional or topical interest and complement or mirror enthusiasts' primary railroads. They have a diversity of equipment and operation and they have some appealing idiosyncrasies. Consider Baltimore & Ohio, Frisco, Milwaukee Road, Boston & Maine.

In the course of reading I found that others, too, admired the Boston & Maine. One of the first articles I encountered in *TRAINS* was David P. Morgan's study of the B&M in the January 1949 issue, "Diesels and Covered Bridges." Years later when I worked with him, he still spoke enthusiastically of the B&M. A photo caption in one of the model railroad magazines back in the 1950s said B&M's maroon and gold diesel paint scheme was one of the prettiest around (surprised me, it did). Hamilton Ellis referred to the B&M in the *Pictorial Encyclopedia of Railways* as "a sort of American South Eastern and Chatham," which may say more about the SE&C than it does about the B&M, to American readers.

There is practically nothing about today's Boston & Maine to connect it with the B&M of the 1940s and

1950s. Lines have been abandoned; others have become short lines; yet others, former New Haven and Boston & Albany lines, have been added to the B&M.

Here are some statistics for 1955, the last full year before Patrick B. McGinnis took over the road. B&M operated 1,574 route miles with 14 steam locomotives and 252 diesel locomotives (not counting B units, and I think there were 29 of those). B&M owned 5,432 freight cars, 642 passenger cars (72 of them self propelled), one articulated streamlined train, and 673 company service cars—and had 10,571 employees. In 1955 it ran off 2,963,731 revenue freight train miles and 5,892,511 revenue passenger train miles (just about twice as many as freight). Average earnings per freight train mile were $22.39; passenger $1.70. It carried 13,966,613 passengers, and the 7,974,484 of those who were commuters are reflected in the average trip, 25.41 miles. It originated 148,892 carloads of freight and received 487,237 carloads from connections. It posted an operating ratio of 76.51 percent.

It was a small railroad and a good one. Come along now and enjoy it with Robert Jones. If it is not your first railroad, it may well become your second.

ACKNOWLEDGEMENTS

Creating this book has been a lifelong dream, and like so many endeavors in our lives, it has been done with the help and guidance of many interested friends.

I believe that the first round of thanks should go to the stalwart photographers whose work appears here, the hardy gentlemen who braved the elements, drove and hiked many miles to create the perfect shot, and who waited patiently at trackside for what to us is that most glorious of all prizes—*the train:*

Wayne D. Allen
Jack Armstrong
David C. Bartlett
Norton D. Clark
Stanley W. Cook
H. Bentley Crouch
T. J. Donahue
Art Forrestal
Dana R. Goodwin
Dick Hamilton
Donald G. Hills
Stephen B. Horsley
Preston S. Johnson
John F. Kane
Walter S. Kowall
J. Emmons Lancaster
Arthur E. Mitchell
George Melvin
Russell F. Munroe

Leon Onofri
Charles G. Parsons
Stephen R. Payne
Ben Perry
Arthur Purchase
Donald S. Robinson
Herman Shaner
Jim Shaughnessy
Dwight A. Smith
Stanley Smith
Joseph Snopek
Dana A. Story
Richard Story
Allan W. Styffe
Edgar A. Swift
Richard W. Symmes
Tom Travers
Peter D. Victory
Woronoff Air Photo Service

I wish to offer a special note of thanks to the following colleagues:
• Preston S. Johnson, whose long career as a B&M dispatcher helped enormously in providing much detail.
• Richard W. Symmes, a friend since high school who unfailingly provided a sympathetic ear and helped with information about the railroad, and who offered helpful evaluation of the manuscript.
• Stanley W. Cook, the first photographer to cooperate in the project and lend his slides to a stranger in California.
• Harry A. Frye, B&M Historical Society Historian, for answering many questions and for reviewing the manuscript and offering invaluable advice.
• H. Arnold Wilder, the eloquent B&M raconteur whose

years of railfanning and observation figured importantly in the review of the manuscript.
• Russell F. Munroe, always gracious in answering questions and offering his slides.
• Donald S. Robinson, whose encyclopedic knowledge of the B&M helped plug many holes in the data.
• David Lamson, for providing information about Bill Sveda, former B&M signal maintainer.
• Joseph Shaw, who helped the author track down several obscure photographs.
• Robert Allen, Dave Johnson, and Ray Tobey for their time and effort in sharing black and white material which, in the end, we could not use because of space limitations.
• Ron Johnson, for the inspiration of his own fine books, and his suggestions about possible contributors here.
• Bob Buck, for assisting at the eleventh hour with suggestions of additional contributors.
• Lester Stephenson, for courtesies at North Station.
• William P. Nixon, the Onofri family, and Bob Liljestrand for loaning material from their collections.
• Last, yet perhaps most important, I must acknowledge the tremendous debt I owe to the Boston & Maine Railroad Historical Society for the prodigious accomplishment of their quarterly *B&M Bulletin* in documenting, in words and photographs, so much of the history of the railroad. These materials were of considerable help to me in assembling this book.

Pacific 3709 with a northbound commuter at Winchester in July 1954. T. J. Donahue photo.

INTRODUCTION

This book is a reminiscence, a fond memory about a fine railroad in New England, the Boston & Maine. Former B&M Signal Maintainer David Lamson described the road as "a group of exceptional men who were members of the B&M family. As a family, we all tried to keep the B&M as efficient and profitable as possible but with a human touch so that all who came in contact with our railroad would know that they were dealing with professionals."

In parts I and IX I have shared my memories as a boy growing up on a quiet branch of the B&M. I suspect they are probably very much like your own memories, and I hope that by including them here I help you to recall those innocent childhood days when trains were new to you.

The historical information in Parts II through VIII is provided to give a general idea about the origin of each line. To help you through these there is a system map on the front endsheet, plus a more detailed map in each of the five major sections. The reader will understand that behind the brief statements relating the dates of chartering, building, opening, operating, merging, and (sadly) sometimes abandoning, there are myriad details of cause and effect, often entailing greed and political intrigue, that—for all the juiciness of the available facts—must be left to the as yet unwritten comprehensive history of the Boston & Maine. It still must be said, though, that a good deal of the trackage absorbed into the B&M as it existed in the early 1900s should never have been built. Because of the excessive, vicious competition of the last century, many people's resources were wasted on virtually useless railroad lines. We often speak of New England branch lines as somehow having lost all their earlier business, that they were profitable when built. Perhaps some were, but consider a statement by the Fitchburg Railroad in their 1856 Annual Report: "in our opinion, the Boston railroads would be far better off if every branch was at once discontinued and iron taken up." And yet, had not the internal combustion engine been invented, one might conjecture that all the overbuilding would have been seen as a great act of foresight in providing a comprehensive transportation network. But American entrepreneurial success with the auto saw to it that the concept was supplanted.

The Boston & Maine was a business. It functioned properly when it could make money. When it couldn't, service was cut back. If conditions didn't subsequently improve, track was taken up. That the B&M was not able to shed unprofitable lines sooner was partly responsible for the road's chronic poor health.

Nonetheless, every foot of track on the B&M, mainline or branch, rain or shine, needed or not, was the scene of legitimate human endeavor, the daily earning of keep, the conducting of commerce. I have ventured to paint its portrait here, and what a subject it was! The space in parts II through VIII is devoted to the best color photographs of the Boston & Maine I could find (most, but not all branches are represented; the availability of good photography was the critical factor). Of the 3,000 plus slides scrutinized during the past three years, some 1,000 were borrowed from their owners. From these, I and my invaluable colleague at Interurban Press, Paul Hammond, chose the material you see here. The choices were very difficult to make; we could have used all of them but the book would have to cost $300 and we might have sold half a dozen. The icy hand of economic reality is no less real in the publishing milieu than it is in that of railroading.

What you see here is a generous representation of operation of the Boston & Maine from the mid 1940s through the mid 1970s. A little stretching on either end has permitted me to include such jewels as Norton D. Clark's photograph of Hoosac Tunnel electrics, Stanley Smith's early Kodachrome of a 10-car *East Wind* in its magnificent yellow and silver garb behind an R-1-D, and the late Richard Story's majestic portrait of a late afternoon freight in the White Mountains.

Every picture in this book tells its own special story. Savor each one, friend, as you embrace this glorious past.

Robert Willoughby Jones
Silverlake
October 1990

I
A BOY ON THE BOSTON & MAINE

I cannot remember my first train; all that I recall is from my earliest awareness I was transfixed by trains, particularly passenger trains. As a little child riding with Mom and Dad in the car I became riveted whenever I saw one through the car window. I spent my boyhood peering out that back window, ever on the alert for a train, eventually becoming very adept at the telltale signs, like the sulfurous smell of steam engine exhaust, roads rising to go over little bridges with tracks hidden below, or telegraph poles and wires peeking beyond a row of trees. As we drove around the North Shore of Boston on weekends, I gradually learned the location of grade crossings—some with electric gates but still many with manned crossing shanties—bridges, semaphores and target signals, and especially the ubiquitous red-brown and ocher colored B&M stations and freight houses, resplendent with baggage carts, railway express vans, bay windows and order boards. The variations in architecture were wonderful, yet you always knew when a building was a railroad station. They were unique unto themselves.

Now and again we drove through Essex, a simple but beautiful town located on the marsh in the tidal basin between Gloucester and Ipswich, and we would always pass this one little white house which I thought looked like a train station. The style was so similar to many others I had seen, and the more I saw it, the more I became convinced that it once had been a station, even though there were no other signs of a railroad, and it was clearly now a residence. One afternoon while in

high school, several years later, I explored the marsh behind the town, and, sure enough, there were remnants of ties and roadbed from the old Essex branch going off toward the house. The house turned out to be Conomo station, at one time the terminus of the branch. Conomo wasn't used after February, 1927, and the last train left the Essex Depot on December 19, 1942. (The track from the entire branch was removed in *one week* because of the war effort. Today the property has been beautifully landscaped, with the house well kept up, but, sad to say, it's one of the few B&M stations to be so lucky.

But I was always in the car it seems, and my Dad was in control, and of course he couldn't be expected to stop for every train or chance of one, though surely my squeals of delight at seeing even a piece of bare track must have kept him constantly on the alert. One Saturday morning when I was four we were driving around Marblehead, my home town, doing errands, when we encountered a live steam engine ready at the head of a Boston bound train. I remember how black the engine was and how conscious I was of the steam everywhere. My Dad, with a nod from the smiling engineer, hoisted me up to the cab where I was given half an oatmeal raisin cookie from him. It was heady attention.

Dad worked in Boston for a real-estate management company, commuting to Boston on the B&M. Until I was four he did so from Marblehead. Then we moved to Topsfield because Mom and Dad wanted their own place in the country, and prices were very reasonable then. Before buying the house, Dad paid a visit to the B&M

B&M Pacific is on its way from Salem into Marblehead, as seen from the Village Street bridge, on a crisp winter morning in 1956, the final *winter season for steam on the railroad. The track at the left is the line to Swampscott and Boston. Russell F. Munroe photo.*

This semaphore in the Castle Hill neighborhood of Salem is where the author had his first lesson in railroad safety. Norton D. Clark photo of June 6, 1955.

Passenger Traffic Department at 150 Causeway Street, Boston, to question them about the likelihood of Topsfield service continuing (this was 1950). There were rumors going around that the B&M was planning to discontinue the Topsfield service. According to my Dad, since the B&M gave him the most rosy picture, he bought the house. A week after we moved in, the Railroad terminated the train to Topsfield. The new highway system was attracting droves of commuters, and the B&M was just beginning the long and draining siege which came within a hair's breadth of doing in its commuter trains. So for the next four years Dad generally drove into Boston on Route 1, though I do remember one wonderful exception.

Occasionally Dad would drive to North Beverly and catch the train there. On one such day, when I was visiting my Grandmother in Salem, he stopped on his way home from Boston to join us for supper, then he took me down to the old stone Salem depot where we caught a steam train. I remember the excitement of holding my head out the open coach window on the right side of the car and watching the locomotive headlight illuminate the dark green pine trees along the way, then their disappearing into the darkness as we rushed past them. I remember, too, the glorious luminosity of the green target signal up ahead, brighter than real, the bracing, cool night air licking my face, the intoxicating sulfury smell from the locomotive, and the crystal stars vibrating on a black glass sky. This was strong stuff for a kid. When I caught a cinder in my eye, my Dad, already a hero this night, got it out with a handkerchief. That ride couldn't have been more than ten minutes in length, but it's been going on in my head ever since.

In the summer of 1954, just after I turned eight, we

moved from Topsfield, via a two-month's stay at Grandma's in Salem, back to Marblehead, this event signalling the real beginning of rail adventure on the B&M. From the moment when Dad first explained to me that we'd be living in Salem for the summer, my thoughts had been about just how and when I could get off on my own to get down to Salem Yard to see the trains by myself. Not from the car window, or with my Dad or grandparents, but alone. As with Christmas, I thought the day would never come.

That first day trackside I learned a valuable lesson about the need to be careful around trains. After reaching the mainline between Salem Yard and the junction of the Marblehead branch, I decided to wait for a train so I could see the semaphore move. These colorful sentinels fascinated me, and though I had spotted dozens of them through the car window, I had never actually seen one *move*. With no train in sight, and looking about for someplace to sit, I decided that the rail looked shiny and clean and a good place to sit while waiting. Trains made a lot of noise, I reasoned, and so I would hear any one which approached.

I became absorbed in my thoughts as I sat waiting, and it was a considerable shock when I looked up and beheld a diesel powered train bearing down on me. Understand that although I surely would have eventually heard it (and we know the alert engineer would have sounded the horn), I had not heard a thing. Not wanting to show the panic I felt and reveal myself to the engineer as a coward, I got up very deliberately and slowly walked over to the signal mast (not so very far from the tracks, you are probably thinking), and leaned against it, all the while trying to look nonchalant. The next few moments scared the living daylights out of me.

My Lord, how the earth did shake as that train flew by. The combination of the force of air and the debris it carried, the deafening sound of that diesel (it was a GP-7 I learned years later), and the sheer physical terror the train instilled in me was a wonderful lesson to learn at an early age. I never had to learn it again, ever since being extremely careful around trains.

Dad had enjoyed commuting on the train and our move to Marblehead enabled him to do so once again. Several times I went into Boston with him on a steam powered train and I recall our stopping briefly at Lynn Tower. He pointed out the window toward a little piece of paper tied to a string that a man in the tower raised up from one of the trainmen. Dad explained that everyday the man in the tower and the crew would exchange riddles and jokes in this way. The crew would pose the question in the morning, while in the evening the tower-man would pass down an answer. It seemed eminently logical.

The need for a pair of new shoes provided the reason for a trip into Boston one warm summer day when I was nine. We went in on Dad's regular morning train and

Lynn Tower on a lazy summer day. Built during the period of New Haven Railroad control in the early 1900s, it reveals its creator's architectural influence. RWJ photo.

walked up to Filene's, which, we discovered, didn't open until 10 a.m., meaning that I would miss the last morning train back to Marblehead. After we bought the shoes, Dad gave me the return portion of my Marblehead ticket and told me to take a train to Salem (he said the fares were identical and that the conductor wouldn't care) and walk up to Grandma Beth's on Lafayette Street and spend the day there. So I got myself down to North Station and took the next train to Salem. For some forgotten reason I got on the Smoker, I think just because I liked the name and I had heard my Grandfather once, when he took me on the train, ask the conductor which way it was. It was very hot by this time, about 11, and all the windows were wide open.

The conductor was furious. He actually yelled at me. "If you've got a *Marblehead* ticket, then *use* it to Marblehead! Do you understand?!" "Yes, sir," I answered quietly. His face was so red I was sure I could see the steam coming out of the sides of his mouth.

It wasn't long before I thought up the idea of walking the mile from our house in Marblehead down to the depot to meet my Dad's train at night. I loved the feel of that old brick station, just being there, watching. I belonged. Soon I decided to meet all four trains, starting at 4:30, because I was so drawn to being around them. When I first started these visits we had a mix of steam and diesel powered trains. The steam locomotives were 4-6-2 Pacifics, and the diesels were always GP-7s, with never an RS-3. Back then, all the trains turned on the wye just beyond the Village Street bridge. There were four afternoon trains, the first and last of which turned on the wye and, after backing into Marblehead station, returned to Boston as revenue trains. The second and third turned on the wye and went to spend the night in the North Street coach yard in Salem. The coming of the Budd Cars changed this routine, replacing in no time the equipment on the first and fourth trains. I first heard about Budd Cars through my Cub Scout Troop, where our leader, Mr. Lancy, told us one day that the B&M was buying them and that there were plans to have some come to Marblehead. There was an animated discussion among the boys about these new trains. We were all excited about their coming to Marblehead. None of us realized it then, but we were witnessing the disappearance of steam from its very last holdout on the B&M, the Marblehead trains.

In the winter months the atmosphere at the depot was sharp and dramatic. It was usually cold and always completely dark when those great, huge, steam powered behemoths came pounding into town spewing smoke and steam. I absorbed every moment of these daily occurences with more pleasure and anticipation than anything else in my life then. I never tired of going to that beautiful old station, of taking in all its glorious artifacts. The lone green roundel in the one-sided order board on the depot roof shone through the blackness like a wise old owl. Never once did I see it red, the sign for a

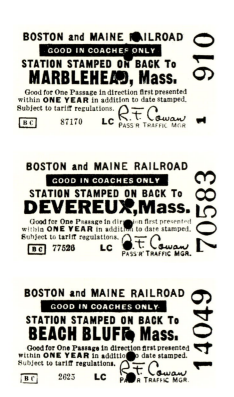

trainman to pick up an order. You could look into the ticket office through the smoky glass of the bay window and see that marvelous wall-mounted lever, locked into the notches, from where the agent controlled the semaphore arm. The lever moved the semaphore by way of some 25 feet of metal pipe, its mechanical design cleverly arranged to go around corners. How I longed to grab hold of that lever and raise the semaphore.

By the time my family actually moved into the new house in Marblehead, school had already begun, so it was of course impossible for me to be at the station in the mornings, and I had to be content with train watching later in the day. When the next summer came, though, I was free all day, and one morning in late June I found myself at the station. My idea was to take a train to Devereux Station, a scant mile from the one in Marblehead, and walk back. Somehow I suspected that this would not cost very much and I was sure I could manage it.

The ticket agent, who introduced himself as Sam Goodwin, was a neat old guy with a sparkle in his eye, and he told me the fare to Devereux was a dime. Handing me the ticket, "You know," he said, his eyes still twinkling over his bifocals, "You can ride all the way to Swampscott on that ticket." That delicious idea certainly opened up a whole new world for me as I considered the possibilities. I did get off that morning at Devereux, because there wasn't to be a return train from Swampscott for some six hours, but as I walked the tracks back to Marblehead on that quiet and peaceful right of way, past the freshly hung laundry in backyards of families I didn't know, I devised a plan.

I would take an afternoon train to Swampscott for the bargain price of 10c, wait for my Dad's train and ride home with him. This would provide two great rides on the train with extra time at Swampscott to watch other trains. The effect of thinking up this plan was like touching a nerve; I was almost fibrillating. And it was so simple. And cheap; logic told me I needed only 20c for this plan. Because I wanted to surprise my Dad with my appearance at seatside onboard his train at Swampscott, I couldn't very well ask him what time his train would pass through there, but I was pretty sure I could figure it out.

The day I chose was bright and sunny, and it was with high spirits of noble adventure that I started off on my junket. To be safe I even went off with a total kitty of 30 cents. I felt very important riding that Budd Car. I was the lone passenger and the train seemed to belong to me. It was a pretty ride through the branch. The scenery was lovely, we went past homes I had never seen before, and the little stations on the line were quaint. The road to Boston went by the stations at Devereux and Phillips Beach, so the family car often passed these, but the stations at Clifton and Beach Bluff were off the beaten track and were therefore new to me. More, the Clifton station was made of stucco, which was unusual. Sure enough, 10 cents got me all the way to Swampscott, site of the junction with the Swampscott Branch and the Eastern Route mainline going to Portsmouth, the Gloucester Branch, and, via Salem, the lines to Peabody and Danvers.

For some reason now forgotten, probably just the thrill of adventure, I wasn't at Swampscott very long before I decided to use my "safety" dime and go on to Lynn (8/10 mile), a seemingly more cosmopolitan location because of its city-like setting and interchange with several of the Eastern Mass bus lines. I duly explored the over-the-street tracks, the street level waiting room and the live ticket agents (notice the plural), and then it was time to catch the Marblehead train and find my Dad. Unfortunately, I couldn't find him on the train, and while I had managed to get through all four cars in the short three minutes between Lynn and Swampscott, you can imagine that I managed really nothing more than a cursory looking over of the passengers. Still, since I had surrendered my last dime, legally I had to get off because 10 cents was not enough fare to get to Marblehead from Lynn. My only hope was that he would be on the next and last train to Marblehead and that *he* could put up the fare.

As I stood on the platform at Swampscott, the precariousness of my position gradually revealed itself to me. If my Dad wasn't on this next train, I imagined a humiliating excoriation by an angry conductor (as you have read, it had happened once before) in front of a train car full of commuters, being forcibly ejected from the train at Phillips Beach and having to walk home four miles from there. Scared and looking for some reassurance, I started a conversation with a man on the platform (about trains, of course) who was most forthcoming about details concerning the three-light home signal guarding the junction. I had become engrossed in watching the target signal with its various color aspects. He explained that only a train for Marblehead would get a bottom green. Some of his explanations were a little beyond me, so I simplified them for my own use. In my system, based on a train's destination, yellow over green over red meant a Danvers train, and so on. He seemed so nice that I confided my financial plight to him, unable to hold back the tears in the process. This kind and reassuring man gave me the 10 cents I needed to get home on the last Marblehead train. Mysteriously, Dad wasn't on that train either. Somebody had given him a lift home that day in a car, as fate would have it.

The shakedown cruise had proven that the journey was indeed possible, if handled with more fiduciary prudence. Dad thought the whole idea amusing and he didn't say no, and soon after I tried it again. Knowing now that he always took the last train, I knew now to wait for it.

I came to love the depot in Swampscott. As the seasons changed, so the place took on different attributes and qualities. In the warm months it stayed light until late, the sun bathing everything in a wonderful orange glow, while in the winter it was bitter blue cold with a faithfully tended pot bellied stove heating the old wooden depot for us seasoned travelers. I never saw anyone tending the fire. It must have been the station agent from the morning trick, there to sell tickets to the hordes of inbound riders. Every day that fire was going. The old station had a lot of character. Always freshly swept inside, it was given a lot of respect by everybody

Depots and places of warm remembrance: **Opposite page**: *Three tickets from the Swampscott Branch and Russell F. Munroe's portrait of a train entering Marblehead.* **Above**: *Stanley W. Cook's October 1953 photo of the Swampscott depot.*

using it. It lived, it functioned, it was *there*. Real. All this was high adventure for a little kid and I remember those days in the mid 1950s with great fondness and warmth.

While in the afternoon the vast majority of passengers using Swampscott arrived from Boston, there were a handful who got on going north. One young nurse (in retrospect, I imagine she was in her 20s; I was 10) would arrive shortly after I did to wait for a Danvers train. She was thin and beautiful and we struck up an immediate friendship. This continued through the fall and into the winter, and I looked forward to seeing her every day. I knew from our conversations that she came in every morning, and, as the Budd Cars began to appear on the scene, becoming more and more numerous, she told me how pleasant they were to ride on. And since I was a fanatic to ferret out any and every detail of train lore, I knew, for example, that she *always* rode in the first car of the train.

Then came that fateful day in February, 1956, when cruel death raised its ugly hand on a B&M morning local from Danvers. In a blinding snowstorm, a six-car train[1] of heavyweight coaches from Portsmouth stopped short of Swampscott station "to secure permission to pass the signal." A four-car Budd train from Danvers, apparently ignoring a red indication on the preceding distant signal (it, too, was reported to have been covered with snow), telescoped into the rear of the Portsmouth train. The engineer, fireman, and eleven passengers were killed. Conductor Walter Roberts was riding near the front of the first car and dove under a seat when the two enginemen frantically entered the passenger section yelling, to warn of the impending collision. He alone survived in that first car.

My Dad's train from Marblehead was stalled on the branch, waiting for a clear signal, just abreast of the wreck site, when he heard the explosion from the impact. He told me the sound was tremendous. Within minutes he could hear the approach of numerous sirens. Later, as refugees from the wrecked trains were herded aboard his train, he overheard ominous conversations about "twisted metal," "wrecked cars," and "blood on the snow." Just imagining the scene is chilling.

Further on into Boston, Dad's train was rear-ended too, though with little of the force of the earlier accident, thank God. The most serious injuries here were whip-lashed necks and wrenched backs. The circumstances were remarkably similar to the earlier accident: a train of Budd RDCs, travelling too fast for conditions, rear ending a conventional steel train. It was a bad, bad day on the Boston & Maine.

My Grandmother was so terrorized by the news of the wreck that she begged my Dad not to ride the train anymore. And since she already took such a dim view of my daily excursions to Swampscott, my Dad thought it would calm her if I were to take a breather for a couple of weeks.

I was afraid for my nurse friend. She was constantly on my mind, but since I had no idea what her name was, the newspaper report of the casualties was useless. The photos of the wreck kept playing in my head. The first Budd Car was obliterated by the impact with the heavyweight coach.

Well, I started the trips again a few weeks later,

and you know, she was there. Her explanation stunned me. Boarding the train in Danvers that morning, reaching the top of the steps, she changed her routine. "I don't know why," she said, "it just came to me to go into the second car for a change." One of life's miracles.

As the Budd Cars became more and more in evidence, the Swampscott Branch benefited. Soon, all the trains to Marblehead were running with Budd equipment. They were beautiful trains and they rode smoothly. They did sway to beat the band, though, and the motors in each car produced a kind of vibration which could give you a headache.

Shortly after I started these trips the crews began to recognize me and, mirabile dictu, refused to take money. The inbound crew knew I loved trains and felt, I guess, some admiration and sympathy. Since Dad was working for the Post Office Department as Regional Real Estate Manager for New England, he travelled on a pass, and they couldn't very well take his kid's last dime, could they? He usually rode in the same seat, the head-end most forward-facing seat on the left side of the forward compartment of the RDC 2. Everyday I would find Dad in his seat, and we each would talk about our days, and he was always unfailingly glad to see me. It meant a lot to me that we had this private time together. From Marblehead Depot the two of us walked home. Up the hill on Pleasant Street we passed the Nichols Funeral Home, where at Christmas time they always had a life-sized display of seven or eight mannequins dressed as carolers on a sleigh ride. Every year I heard the same lecture about how lurid the whole idea was, given their

Left: Unlike many railroad stations, Marblehead's was smack in the middle of town, a focal point for daily activity, seen here with the local fife and drum parade on the way to the annual "Muster," in which rival fire departments of the North Shore would vie to see which could shoot water the farthest, using hand pumps. The Ford dealership in the foreground is on land which earlier carried trains several yards further into town. Russell F. Munroe photo.

business. It always made me laugh to hear him rail on about it.

I rode the train to Swampscott for about two years. I don't remember when I stopped, but eventually I went with other interests. Then, one day in June 1959, about 7 p.m. I was at home when I heard the Budd Car's horn down at the Depot whooping up a storm. Dad said it was the last train out and that there would be no more. Somehow I hadn't even heard it was the end.

It would have killed me to see it, but I should have been there. When you love trains and they abandon your town then rip up the tracks, it's as if a part of you is torn away. For all these years I have had a recurring dream about tracks being relaid and service being restored to Marblehead.

The crossing just ahead of the Marblehead station was protected for years by Louis Davis, a nasty old curmudgeon if ever there was one. He could usually be found, skulking around the property, looking mean. One day when I first started going to the Marblehead depot to meet Dad, before the Swampscott concept had jelled, Louis yelled at me and my brother Geoff, telling us in no uncertain terms to get the hell off the railroad's property. I suppose he thought we were vandals, because some of our contemporaries in town certainly were, but whatever the reason, we were indeed shaken up. My Dad had quite a temper and when Geoff and I gleefully recounted, verbatim, what Louis had said to us, my Dad administered to Louis one of the verbal lashings for which he had become so famous in Post Office circles. Louis did not bother us after that. Eventually, he retired and the B&M arranged that each train's brakeman would flag the crossing. It was only a few feet to the station, the end of the line, and it really was a fairly satisfactory solution, albeit a sad one.

On a typical day I would ride the 5 p.m. (the times varied from timetable to timetable) train to Swampscott and return with my Dad on his train at Swampscott about 6:20, giving me just over an hour of train watching time. There were a fair number of trains then, and the variety of equipment was fascinating and colorful. Unfortunately, I didn't know beans about steam engines, so I didn't register classes or numbers. Diesels were more identifiable to me, but I only remember the GP-7s and the RS-3s. If we ever had a BL-2 I don't remember it.

From the timetable of October 30, 1955:
(I arrive Swampscott at 5:16 p.m., on Train 2220*)

Train No.	Time	Direction	To/From
2219	5:23	outbound	Marblehead
2537	5:27	outbound	Rockport**
243	5:36	outbound	Portsmouth**
2536	5:43	inbound	Rockport* **
2221	5:46	outbound	Marblehead
2539	5:51	outbound	Rockport* **
2418	5:55	inbound	Danvers*
2417	5:57	outbound	Danvers*
251	6:13	outbound	Portsmouth**

(I depart Swampscott at 6:22 p.m., on Train 2223*)
  * Budd Highliner
  ** Did not stop at Swampscott; time is inferred

From my earliest days the diesel that caught my fancy as having *the* look was that of an E unit (7, 8, or 9, though of course I didn't know these designations then) or an F unit. Lionel modeled their O gauge F-3 in this way, such as on their Santa Fe Super Chief. And, in 1954 they introduced a brilliant green paint job, rich and ele-

gant looking, after the prototype on the Southern. I thought diesels like those with the wonderful paint schemes in the Lionel catalogue had a lot of class. On my B&M, though, mostly all I saw were Geeps. My Great Aunt Mary lived in Winchester and sometimes would invite me up to visit, and because she loved the arts she often took me into Boston to plays and concerts. One morning we waited, with a large crowd, on the platform (when Winchester trackage was still at street level) for the Boston train. The agent's voice came over the loudspeaker, announcing that the train would be coming over the Woburn Loop and had nine mail and express cars at the front with the coaches at the rear. At the head of the train was one of the E-7s in that maroon and gold scheme, my first clue that the Railroad owned anything like this. I think it was the only time I ever saw a B&M E-7 on the head end of a passenger train. These patrician beauties virtually never came up to the North Shore, and by the time I started taking photos in 1961, all but 3809 were retired, and it, too, followed in a few months. Its last assignment was the evening milk run to White River Junction over the New Hampshire Division. Later, I photographed many of the E-7s at the Schiavone scrap yard at Mystic Wharf when they went to the big railway in the sky.

Salem

Salem—My memories of railroading in this little city begin when I was about three. The strongest visual image I have is of the double set of wide, yellow and black crossing gates spreading across Canal Street with their little red lights flashing on the bars and their warning signals going "tiddledy, tiddledy." I was struck, too, by those black monoliths with the rounded tops—they looked like gravestones—that you'd see at every crossing shanty. They had cranks on them, turned by the shanty tender to lower the gates. Magically, these men knew when the train was coming long before it could be seen. Just how was a mystery until years later when I learned that each shanty was equipped with an advance warning bell.

We lived in Marblehead then, but my father's parents lived in Salem and since a lot of our shopping was done there, many weekends were spent coming and going through Salem. It was inevitable that I would see trains, those glorious old wine colored cars pulled by steam or diesel and the occasional freight. The imposing Salem depot has stayed with me as a vision of mysterious darkness and moist, weighty stones, full of pigeons and an overwhelming dirtiness, yet an absolutely mag-

Above: The view from the Salem Tower area in 1954.
Norton D. Clark photo.
Right: Bob Cleary at the Tower in the early 1960s;
notice the flowers to improve the decor. RWJ photo.
Left: The Norman-influenced Salem depot literally
*loomed over the city. This August 1953 view is a fine
period study of the station's environs.*
Arthur E. Mitchell photo.

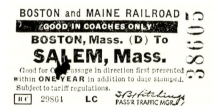

BOSTON and MAINE RAILROAD
GOOD IN COACHES ONLY
BOSTON, Mass. (D) To
SALEM, Mass.
Good for One passage in direction first presented
within **ONE YEAR** in addition to date stamped.
Subject to tariff regulations.
BC   29861   LC   *J. B. Hitchings*
PASS'R TRAFFIC MGR

nificent presence. The old geezers who flagged the front end crossing on Norman Street always wore visored caps and they had bi-directional stop signs, and it took three of them to stop the traffic safely. And I remember most vividly the spring switch and its big identifying metal sign on the side of the tunnel entrance. One day I discovered what a spring switch was, just moments after having covered my eyes to avert seeing what I was sure was going to be a derailment. One of the old crossing tenders explained how it worked: as the single track emerged from the tunnel, dividing into two tracks, the switch was always set so that every train would take the path to the right. The switch was held in this position by a spring rather than by a lock, so that a train going against it the wrong way, into the tunnel, would simply push the switch over with each set of wheels. As the points of the switch moved, the switch stand jerked

around, with the switch lantern getting quite a beating every time. Needless to say, train operation over spring switches must be slow.

A few times I even got to ride on the B&M. Once my Grandma Beth and Grandpa Francis took me to Boston Garden to see the circus on a cold, rainy day in the fall. I can feel our coach slowing on the Lynn marsh for the General Electric drawbridge, and I can see the river below without any sign of a bridge holding the train up. I have merely a vague memory of the circus, but it's just as if it were yesterday that I held my Grandfather's hand as he hurried us through the gate to our return train. In a cloud of steam we slipped up the back steps of the rear coach, the train already moving. Back in Salem late that afternoon in the pouring rain, stepping from the train, I can still see the two green eyes, their illumination reflecting off the slick rails, peering through the

The advance crew awaits the Paul Revere Special in the warmth of the Beverly Depot waiting room: Julius Wasserstram, B&M Police; Frank Wilson, Trainmaster; Jim Heselton, Car Department; Earl Leopold, Carman; Andy Robinson, Sales Representative—Traffic Department. Outside can be seen a Budd RDC9 on an inbound commuter run. RWJ photo.

grayness from the semaphore mast in the yard far south of the depot, showing the way for the next Boston-bound train. And the smell of those old red coaches. Was there ever anything quite like the pungent, musty smell from mold in the car cooked by the steam heat, mingling with the permeating sulfur fumes? I will never forget it.

Scouts to Salem

My Cub Scout Troop sometimes went on field trips. In my second year my Mom was one of two Den Mothers—Lois Hailey was the other—and one of the trips they concocted was to go to Salem to see the engine-house and its turntable and to climb the steps to Salem Tower for a look. In the mid 1950s Salem Tower still had very large, clumsy looking levers to control the signals and track switches. The levers were a good 6″ long and they were no doubt the first generation of electrical equipment following the removal of what originally must have been Armstrong levers. The Towerman, an old gentleman named Bob Cleary, admonished us somewhat sternly not to touch any of the switches. What a wonderful place to work, I remember thinking, with all the

colored lights on the track diagram and the great view one had of the tidal river and down the track to Northey Point. A Geep went by with some red coaches while we were up there, and Mr. Cleary showed us how the lights changed on the track diagram as the train moved into different blocks.

Paul Revere Special

One dark winter night about six o'clock, Lincoln Soule—my best friend and only train watching pal—and I went to Beverly to see B&M President Patrick McGinnis and his retinue hold forth from the rear platform of an observation car as part of a two day train movement, called the *Paul Revere Special,* to sound the alarm about the potential loss of all rail passnger business on the North Shore unless subsidies were forthcoming. Two B&M GP-7s pulled a streamlined New York Central coach, diner, and a heavyweight observation. Trainmaster Frank Wilson[2] was on hand for the occasion, along with several other B&M officials, checking details at the Depot in advance of the train. Their photo is above. Later when the official train arrived, I made some flash pictures of the assembled officials on the rear platform. I remember McGinnis and his colleagues being a little nervous about the popping bulbs; I'm sure I didn't look like a serious photographer at age 15.

The train came in from the north, having joined the Eastern Route at Portsmouth via the Portsmouth Branch from Rockingham Junction. After a public session with speeches in front of the depot, with a crowd of perhaps 15 persons, the train backed onto the siding on the north side of Beverly Depot. An attendant put out a welcoming sign and the local dignitaries went on board for drinks and a little arm squeezing.

My being out on my bicycle after dark used to drive my Dad wild. And in the wintertime, he didn't get much argument from me. Riding the bike in January was especially difficult, not only because it was bitter cold, but because there was a lot of snow on the ground, making the roads narrower, and my bicycle forays were much truncated in the cold months. The saviour on this occasion was Lincoln's Mom, who drove us safely to Beverly, waited and kept the car warm while we had our encounter with *Paul Revere*.

Winchester

My Great Aunt Mary lived in Winchester, a 45 minute drive from Marblehead. Our family sometimes joined Aunt Mary there for a service at the First Congregational Church. They tried packing me off to Sunday School the first couple of times, but I asked if I mightn't accompany them to the main service because the music there with the large choir and the organ so appealed to me. My Dad hated organized religion so

The author's first train photo. A B&M GP-7 pulls two RDCs through the fresh snow at Winchester on February 5, 1961.

much that he mentally counted the patterns on the ceiling or in the ornate lamps to pass the time. The formal dogma didn't much interest me either, but I was passionate about the music. I loved going to church there, in no small part because the building sat high on a hill overlooking the B&M mainline and its passenger station. Trains were coming and going constantly, and there was a lot to see. Through passenger trains for White River Junction and Montreal, trains to Laconia and the Lake Winnepesaukee region, and local trains for the Woburn Loop and Lowell all called at Winchester, and of course there were numerous freights as well. I wasn't around to see a great deal, but what I did see whet my appetite for when I eventually was old enough to take Aunt Mary's bike and go off on my own with the camera to stalk trains.

One night I got special permission from Aunt Mary to be out after dark and I went down to the tower[3] to make friends with the man on duty, Arthur Bohnwagner. A great guy with a saucy sense of humor, he didn't mind answering the thousand questions from a train-crazy kid. After I'd observed him on a few visits and gotten the feel of running the board, I asked if I could try it alone. So one night while I ran the trains at Winchester, he sat by, monitoring my moves. Any phone or radio communications he handled.

Two towers with which I became familiar, Winchester and Salem, shared a similarity. The local territory of each board was controlled by what was called "direct wire," whereby you were in direct control, via the switches on the board, of the relay devices which activated the track switches and signals. The more distant territory was controlled by "code." Here, the switch on the board activated a simple computer operation which used a common wire for all the track switches and signals down the line. Since the code method took a minute or two to unwind and complete its machinations, train directors would occasionally do the lining up of track switches and signals on their board, waiting to push the activating button until they were sure this was the appropriate move. For example, if you did not know whether a westbound or an eastbound train was going to reach a particular section of single track first, you might line up the probable move while awaiting the actual appearance of a train (a red light came on in the block occupied by the train, and a bell sounded in the tower whenever a new train entered the tower's controlling territory), before executing the move.

One night Arthur was absorbed in some reading, and after lining up a move for an inbound freight due in about 30 minutes, he went back to his reading. He didn't remember to activate the move, and the freight didn't get its green signal as it moved south toward the junction at Winchester. The train got slower and slower, its diesels grinding loudly in the distance. Finally, four nasty whistle blasts from the engineer got Arthur's attention. He was very serious about his work, and this embarrassed him. This was the only time I ever saw a train director make a mistake, and of course there had been no actual danger, just inconvenience.

My first train photos were taken at Winchester. I had bought opera tickets for me and my Aunt as Christmas presents to us. We were to see Bizet's *Carmen* on February 4, 1961, but after an enormous blizzard raged all day we were forced to cancel our trip to Boston on the train, because they were running only sporadically, and my Aunt was afraid there wouldn't be a return train later that night. The next morning the snow lay white and glistening in the bright sun. I borrowed my Aunt's Brownie camera and a roll of film, and after taking a shot of her beautiful stucco house I headed off for the B&M tracks. The Railroad used various types of equipment to clear snow, depending on the heaviness. Generally, Budd Cars could not, by themselves, cope with snow and, like diesels, they couldn't function through any depth of water, either. My first ever train shot depicts a GP-7 moving past me at the junction of the Woburn Loop in Winchester towing two Budd Cars. It must have been moving at about 50 mph, which is why, as one can see, the Brownie didn't stop the action with its 1/60 second shutter speed. A pair of F-2As subsequently went up the Loop and ran through the switches at the junction. Considerable snow packed on the front gave a hint of some of the snow banks they must have gone through.

North of Winchester about a mile is a section called Winchester Highlands. There a signal bridge spans the two mainline tracks, and I, railroad photographer newly armed with Brownie equipment, thought it would be adventurous to climb it. After hiking up to the bridge and climbing up on top, where the height made it more than a little scary, I took one picture and got down. It was just too cold up there in the wind, and Lord only knows how long I would have waited for a train.

Winchester had it all: local and express trains, passenger and freight trains, and plenty of signals and switches protecting the junction. New, heavy rail and an immaculate look to the roadbed were products of the then recently completed grade separation project. The new waiting room, platforms and ramps, though sterile and completely without the charm of the old depot, were at least clean and functional, unlike a dump, say, like Lynn. For the town of Winchester, though, the grade separation project was a trade-off. The hazards of grade crossings disappeared from the lives of its citizens while providing a visual scar in the form of a gigantic concrete monolith right through the middle of this formerly simple village.

After one Sunday of church and afternoon dinner at Aunt Mary's, Dad's return route to Marblehead took us through the center of Woburn, past its ornate brick depot. As we crossed the tracks by the depot in the darkness, I could see the crossing tender poised at the gates, his hands just beginning to turn the cranks. The

The Talgo heads into Salem Tunnel. RWJ photo.

gates moved inward as we passed through them. I could see a headlight in the distance to the south, and passengers waiting anxiously on the station platform, casting long shadows from the platform lights. Had I seen an agent pulling a Railway Express cart up the platform, looking over his shoulder for the train? All of this I saw in a flash, my head spinning with excitement. I was too scared to ask if we could stop. It was probably nothing more exciting that the 7:15 local from Boston to Lowell via the Woburn Loop, but what a sense of drama and atmosphere it all provided. How impressionable a child is.

My Early Photography

Because my time at taking train photos was limited, I would shoot whatever was there when I arrived at a destination. That is why, if I were on, say, a car trip with my Dad on our way to Rutland, Vermont, and he stopped so I could shoot a station or a car on a siding, or whatever, it was common not to have more than a minute or two. I almost never had advance knowledge of freight train schedules.

Thus, many of my own pictures are not action photos but shots of buildings or locations, or stationary trains. One pleasant result is that sometimes I recorded things which others did not. Also, for me, film was expensive. I hadn't much cash, so I tried not to waste pictures. Looking back, I wish I had taken dozens more, but there it is.

School was another restriction on railroad photography. Winter days in the Northeast are very short and the light fades early on. As soon as I learned about the Talgo Train, for example, I wanted to photograph it, but because it came through Salem every day just before 6 p.m., it was only possible to get good light during the summer. If I went to Salem on the bike during the winter (I am speaking of the cold months from October through April) on a school day, that would mean arriving about 3:30 at the earliest. Weekends, of course, were a different story, but the Talgo didn't run then.

I discovered the Talgo quite by accident. Dad and I were driving past Salem Tower one morning when there it was, on its way inbound, heading into the tunnel. I had no idea the B&M owned any passenger equipment other than Budd Cars. To my pleading for an explanation Dad replied ever so casually, "Oh, that's the Talgo Train, one of McGinnis's stupid ideas." It may have been a stupid idea, but it certainly was different. At least I hadn't heard of it before. And so, one morning I was up earlier than usual to get to Salem on my bike before 7:44 a.m. when the train would pass into the tunnel. Except for the "telltale" getting in the way, stripped of its warning wires, it's a fine shot. If you look carefully at any photograph of the Talgo, you will notice a skirting of dirt on the lower portion of the cars. This resulted

from the brushes on the car washer at Boston Engine Terminal being too high for the train, designed as they were for more conventional equipment. Another idiosyncracy of the Talgo was that for the whole time I chased it over many months, the southernmost car had a flat wheel which banged loudly, and I don't know if it ever was repaired. Carl Kenerson, one of several engineers who ran it, told me that the two Fairbanks Morse diesels on the Talgo were wonderful to operate, but that neighbors at the end of the line complained bitterly about the loud engines running all night. So the Talgo went from home to home like the obstreperous foster child.

Rockingham Racer

Winchester exhilarated me. It had a sense of action which the line through Salem lacked. Where a freight through Salem might have ten or fifteen cars, one through Winchester might have a hundred and be headed up by three or four diesel units. Winchester had a busy junction, and a lot of signals everywhere which were always illuminated, rather than "approach lit." There were express passenger trains which bypassed Winchester at 70 mph (Well, it *seemed* like 70), while at Salem every train stopped, or at least slowed for the tunnel.

During one warm and lazy summer afternoon, as I walked below the tracks at Winchester just a half hour or so past noon, an eight car Budd train highballed

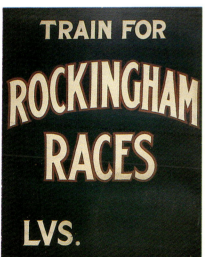

Below: An eight-car Rockingham Racer *highballing over Winchester, Massachusetts in the summer of 1961, its last season of operation. At* **left** *is its colorful roll sign from North Station. The gate attendant would chalk in the appropriate departure time. Both, RWJ photos.*

north. What could this be, I wondered, since at that hour the most one usually saw was a pair of Budds, and that was rare, a lone RDC being the norm. Back at Winchester Tower Arthur Bohnwagner told me it was the *Rockingham Racer*, bound for Rockingham Park in Salem, New Hampshire. The next day I was ready. I had created the picture in my mind: the train framed by the red target signals on the signal bridge. I knew I would have to use the maximum 1/500 second shutter speed on my new camera. The shot came out well; I've always been proud of it. It's the only shot I've ever seen of a regularly scheduled B&M train with this many Budd Cars in mid-day. It was common enough in rush-hour on the Reading line, but never with the sun over-head. Strangely, I never saw the return version of the train, which passed through Winchester just before 7 p.m. Author Ralph E. Fisher has a saucy phrase for the train in his *Vanishing Markers:* "They went up with a trainload of hopefuls and came back with a trainload of long faces." By the time I photographed the train in 1961, it was down to a single section, and this proved to be its last year. Earlier, in 1958, the train had run in two sections, according to an advertisement in the timetable. Reportedly the train was taken off because of patrons having too much to drink and causing damage. I liked it because it was new and different and flashy. It was very easy to become bored with small Budd Car trains. So much alike.

Lynn Tower and Eddie Snow

In its heyday, Lynn Tower must have been a fasci-nating point of operation. Its main floor, two stories above the track, was quite large, about 24 feet by 48 feet, and no doubt accommodated hundreds of Armstrong levers. When the tower at West Lynn was taken out of service, its jurisdiction was given to Lynn Tower. This territory now started with the General Electric draw-bridge (10.5 miles from Boston) and ended north of Swampscott station at the junction of the branch going off to Marblehead (12.8 miles from Boston), a total dis-tance of just over two miles. In between were numerous freight sidings, the junction with the north end of the Saugus Branch, the short section of four-track mainline around Lynn station—added when the B&M was under the ownership of the New Haven in the early 1900s, and two other stations, East Lynn and Swampscott.

When I first ventured into Lynn Tower in 1961, the automatic train board sat in the middle of an enormous room. Outside it was a hot, bright day, but inside it was much darker, the window shades drawn down halfway to keep the hot sun out, and most of the lower portions of the many windows were raised. Seated at the board was one of the true relics of B&M railroading, Eddie Snow. He was a thin lipped, reedy voiced, white haired sep-tuagenarian from West Peabody who was friendly in a reserved, gentlemanly way, and a little crusty in the

bargain. Lynn Tower had one peculiar feature which I never saw anywhere else on the Railroad. Most order boards were installed on a station roof. At Lynn, a pair were installed, one over the other, on the side of the building. An adjacent bridge for road traffic would have obscured the signals from being seen from the north had they been on the roof. The order board signal controlling southbound traffic had its blade mounted in an unusual fashion in relation to the colored glass roundels so that it could turn without hitting the side of the building. This close positioning was probably also the result of tight space between the track and the tower. Semaphores fascinate. Why is this? Perhaps they hark back to our apparent love of heraldry and banners, but there is no question that they do fire the imagination. Every time I visited Lynn Tower, Ed Snow let me work those order board semaphores. I surely must have done this five or six times, and each time I would ask new questions dreamed up to glean yet more information about the railroad, all the while getting up enough courage to say "Would it be okay if I tried the signal today?" "Why, yes, I think that would be alright" was always the quiet, gentle reply. I believe and hope that he understood the drives of one obsessed with trains. If memory serves me, Ed Snow held the only trick at Lynn Tower in those years, from 7 a.m. to 3 p.m. All that was left of the once busy territory was a freight siding for the West Lynn Creamery and the switches to the north end of the Saugus Branch which lost its passenger ser-vice (two rush hour trains each way) in 1958. By the time of my visits there was no more service to Marblehead, and one of the four tracks at Lynn station had been embargoed. When Ed left at three, he set up the switches for automatic operation. The day came, I suppose, when Ed retired and the Railroad simply left the Tower in automatic operation. Today there's just a barren spot by the tracks where this wonderful stucco tower once stood.

And yes, it had been Ed Snow giving train orders for the Marblehead trains to go down the unsignalled Swampscott Branch. He would have liked my Dad, for he really got a chuckle when I told him Dad's explana-tion of the note on the string.

On my second visit to the tower, Ed Snow was a lit-tle cool toward me. I didn't understand at first but after a few minutes of heavy atmosphere he opened up. It seems that during my first visit I had washed my hands in the sink to get rid of the grime from a long bike ride and climbing around Lynn station, and I left a residue of dirt on the porcelain from not rinsing it properly. Well, I apologized and he forgave me, and it did make me more aware of such things for the future.

Ed Snow had been on duty the morning of the Swampscott wreck in 1956, the incident having taken place in his jurisdiction. Actually, the Portsmouth train's conductor was phoning for permission to proceed past the home signal which began Lynn Tower's west-

Just past 12:00 noon, one of two Salem switchers heads into the tunnel, from Peabody enroute to Salem Yard where the men will pause for lunch. Ten minutes later the second switcher will follow. RWJ photo.

bound (south by actual direction) territory when the collision occurred. This was one of those events on the Railroad about which, horrifying as it was, I always wanted to know more details. Ed had excellent recall of the circumstances, and, of course, it had only happened five years earlier.

Lynn station was a desolate affair. The offices for passenger ticketing and the stationmaster were located at street level in a post-war aluminum looking building which was clearly not being cared for. Access to the passenger platforms was by means of rusting iron stairways, with water often dripping down from above, and it was never properly lighted. Really, Lynn station was bleak and charmless.

Lynn did have the convenience of bus connections to Boston, and although it was much simpler, faster, and cheaper to board a bus at the foot of Pearl Street in Marblehead where I lived, and to stay on the bus all the way to Haymarket Square in Boston, anyone seriously afflicted with train disease will instantly recognize the pure, simple logic of de-bussing at Lynn to ascend the rusty stairs and wait twenty five minutes in the extreme

hot or cold (up high on the platform one was at the mercy of the elements) for a Budd Car ride to Boston.

The Salem Tunnel

They say that the 1954, $7 million tunnel project killed Salem. It seemed as if they would never finish the construction, and it went on for a good four years. When it was finally done in 1958, Salem's downtown shopping business was a shambles. To avoid the traffic and parking snarls which became commonplace, people looked elsewhere to shop. And, as fate would have it, on a gentle sloping grassy hill in Peabody, next to Route 128, a new idea came to fruition in those years: the shopping center. Then, the Northshore (as they spelled it) Shopping Center was a jewel of a place, the latest thing, where everyone wanted to go for their shopping. Now, compared to its younger siblings which have continued to sprout in the ensuing years, it has begun to look old and tired.

The tunnel project, similar to a counterpart grade separation in Winchester (which went over instead of

The engineer's view from GP-7 1566 on its way up the Gloucester Branch this fine summer day in 1961. RWJ photo.

under), undertaken at about the same time, eliminated two nasty grade crossings[4]. The City of Salem eagerly joined the Boston & Maine in facilitating the project, and so it came to be. Down came the famous, magnificent Norman castle and in its place came a parking lot. The new depot was a utilitarian building with a comfortable, if small, waiting room with accompanying restrooms, just across Mill Street from the old depot. One reached the tracks by way of very steep and long stairs which could wind anyone over 15, and which were roundly condemned by all for being inconsiderate and unfortunate in design. There was an elevator on the westbound side but it was not frequently used.

For a long time I was afraid to venture into the tunnel, no doubt the best attitude to have about such a place, but eventually I did go in on two or three occasions to take photos, but only after ascertaining from the train director at the Tower just what movements to expect (Also, I certainly didn't explain what I was up to, or it surely would have been forbidden). Actually, the north end of the tunnel was quite safe, because there was considerable room inside, between the diverging tracks to Peabody and Beverly.

At 1:30 in the morning of Tuesday, January 31, 1961, a 20-inch water main on Bridge Street snapped from the cold, releasing 5 million gallons of water, much of

which made its way into the tunnel to a depth as high as ten feet. So strong was the fear of the water freezing in the tunnel that boats were rowed to prevent it, according to the *Boston Herald*.

Portsmouth and Rockport trains were rerouted through Wakefield Junction, while Salem and Beverly passengers detrained at Swampscott and took special busses. Fortunately, quick action by the local workmen enabled normal service to be resumed by mid-day on Wednesday.

Up the Gloucester Branch on the *Camel*

My first actual experience riding an engine happened in Salem Yard. I became friendly with the crew of one of the two switchers and they invited me to ride with them onto the Marblehead Branch while they dropped a car at New England Coke, a quarter of a mile up the branch. Beyond New England Coke there were some small customers on the Salem portion of the branch, but once into Marblehead, it was just great scenery until Bessom Street where Gilbert and Cole Lumber Co. was located. By this time, 1961, Gilbert and Cole had finally given up being Marblehead's only freight customer, so the switcher no longer had any reason to go there. Too bad, for I really would have liked to ride those tracks.

Riding the switcher whetted my appetite for grander ventures.

Burr Town, the patient, friendly train director at Salem Tower, was the one who explained all about the local freight trains. The *Camel* was scheduled to leave Boston at 5 a.m. to go up and back on the Gloucester Branch on Monday, Wednesday, and Friday, while on Tuesday and Thursday it turned at Salem. The *Oil Extra* went up the Danvers Branch to Topsfield on Monday through Friday, leaving Boston at 1:30 p.m. The *Portsmouth Freight* went to that city on a two-day out and back schedule, going north at 2:15 a.m. from Boston on Tuesday, Thursday, and Saturday, usually returning in mid-morning the following day. The motive power for each of these freights was strangely consistent. A GP-7 always led the *Camel*, an Alco RS-3 the *Oil Extra*, with usually a GP-7 for the *Portsmouth Freight*, though once while waiting at Pickman Park on a foggy, hazy afternoon I saw the last named train headed up by a "Bluebird"—one of the B&M's newest Geeps, the product of a GM trade-in of the old wartime FTs. Freight trains were designated in the Freight Train Symbol Book "showing symbol indications, approximate schedule and class of freight to be handled by regular freight trains... The times herein mentioned are not guaranteed...". Thus, while the *Camel* was scheduled to leave Boston at 5 a.m., because of varying business on the way, it could be expected to appear in Salem anywhere between 8 and 10 a.m.

My second ride in a locomotive cab was an extended one: I joined the crew of the *Camel* for a trip up and back from Salem on the Gloucester Branch. Another summer had come and I had become friendly with the crew by talking with them now and again when they'd be in Salem putting their train together in the afternoon for Boston. Eventually I asked about riding in the cab. I was urged to talk to Paul Abbott, the engineer. "Yeah, that'd be OK," he said, "what about next Wednesday?"

It was just like waiting for Christmas, only it was summer. Wednesday came. Another cold, overcast day on the north shore. Too bad, for I had envisioned an azure day for this special trip. I biked over to Salem, leaving the bike in the freight house, and we were on our way by 9 a.m. What a thrill to be in the cab of B&M Geep 1566, its maroon and gold paint still looking sharp. In a diesel cab you are high off the ground. If you travel on trackage you already know, you see many familiar sights from an entirely different perspective. The target signals are lit from the moment you spot them, say, coming around a curve. If you did not know that they went out after you passed them, you would think they stayed lit. You see, far ahead, that the crossing signals are operating to stop traffic. Where a motorist sees flashing

red lights, the cab crew sees smaller, white lights facing the track. This trip was also the first time I actually could see things inside Salem tunnel. When you went through on a passenger train, all you could see in the window was the reflection of everything in the car because of the reading lights. There weren't any lights in the cab and the headlight was on, so you could see every detail on the tracks and the dankly moist, gray walls. At Beverly, the depot seemed low in comparison to when I had stood next to it, and encountering the switches and the diamond at Beverly Junction was a real kick, too.

Soon we were at Gloucester Crossing, actually Cabot Street in Beverly, with the last hand operated crossing gate on the B&M. The quaint, slightly beat-up little depot at Montserrat recalled many earlier hours of childhood where we Jones kids played with our friends the Gardners in the mid fifties (I saw my first "American Flyer" coach on this spot). Then into the thick summer foliage so prevalent in Massachusetts. On through Paradise Crossing as the sun broke through the clouds, coming as a nice surprise after I had resigned myself that a cab ride on an overcast Gloucester Branch was better than no cab ride at all. Prides Crossing, of

The Camel waits in the hole while an afternoon RDC local drifts by. The author was riding the caboose. RWJ photo.

course, remains the quintessential New England railway setting. There was a cross-hatched wooden fence there unlike any other I'd seen. Then a short hop to Beverly Farms where the station still functioned as a station. Finally at Manchester we pulled off the main to drop a freight car on a siding, but before switching we waited for a northbound Budd Car to pass. There were occasional sidings to be worked from here on into Gloucester. We got off the main there while switching cars just above the station, and after that same Budd Car came south on its return trip to Boston, we parked the diesel in front of the depot for a 45 minute lunch at a nearby sandwich counter.

Railroad people are pretty down to earth types. They're usually hardy, able to work long hours, and strong. They climb around cars, throw switches, run ahead of engines to keep things moving, and they have instincts like athletes. All that I ever met liked working on the railroad as a line of work. Most were not rail-fans, let alone inebriated with the *idea* of trains as I was, but they did appreciate the craft of operating a railroad well. After lunch Paul Abbott, using my camera, took my picture sitting in the cab. I looked so serious.

Now up to Rockport and its little loop with its ancient and simple hand operated interlocking and semaphores. We turned the diesel on the loop to keep the short end of 1566 forward for the return trip. There were a few cars to be switched at Rockport as well. There was a fine old depot there with a dilapidated one-sided order board. Five minutes' walk away were the harbor and dozens of interesting shops and galleries in Rockport's art colony on Bearskin Neck.

Because we had done all the switching work on the outbound trip, we ran express all the way to Salem on the inbound. Though it was hot, there were occasional breezes off the water which one did indeed feel whenever we got close. We were back in Salem by 3:30. I thanked all the crew and headed home on the bike, very satisfied and content, completely fulfilled by this invigorating day on the *Camel*.

Two weeks later I asked if I could do it again, but this time to ride in the caboose. It occurred to me that the perspective would be very different, and I hoped the crew would agree. At first there were a few raised eyebrows and wary glances exchanged, but they went along with it. Two days later I was off again for another trip to Rockport on the *Camel*.

The interior of a caboose is ever so slightly grimy.

Above: Engineer Paul Abbott snapped this shot of the author aboard 1566 at Gloucester.

Right: Rockport depot was in poor shape, yet it still clearly showed the simplicity and dignity of its design. RWJ photo.

There are the ubiquitous clippings from what Dad called "girlie" calendars, a toilet you'd like to take some Lysol and a wire brush to, and a stove. And very hard seats.

Standing out vividly in my mind is the return part of this trip, where I rode, with the conductor's permission, on the rear platform of the caboose. I thought of it as a poor man's observation car. You saw the world, or at least that portion of it between Rockport and Salem, Massachusetts, in a milieu that precious few others had the chance to see. Sometimes the dust would swirl around the end of the car, drying out my eyes. And I felt especially important at crossings where traffic was held back while my train passed. Being out there you could see things beautifully, whereas the windows in the caboose were small and dirty, and since it was one of the B&M C150 series cabooses for short runs (rebuilt in 1959 from wooden, Laconia-built cabooses), there was no cupola. Every so often the conductor came out to see if I was still on the car and to remind me to hold on. As I look back on these trips, I marvel at how evenly these men treated me, and how much they trusted me. I hope some of you men are still on this earth and that you can know how much you did for a wide-eyed kid from Marblehead.

The Jelly Factory and White River Junction

My Great Aunt Mary learned early on in her life how to drive a car, while her older sister Elizabeth, who never did, complained bitterly about this inability until the day she died. Mary's livelihood depended on having a car to get to and from work and in her day work was sometimes very far afield. Her first teaching job, for example, was in Laconia, New Hampshire. She spent her entire teaching career dealing with "special" students (read horrible and obnoxious). My Father always believed that the repeated annual waves of these monsters are what made Auntie Mae, as she was called, the nervous wreck she became. (Probably what caused her to go really bonkers in the early seventies was a head injury sustained from falling off a top bunk in third class aboard a tourist liner to Majorca in 1958. But I digress.)

Mary, with car, would frequently organize trips for herself and her sister, Elizabeth, my maternal Grandmother. While they did venture as far as California in 1946—and Beth's reminiscences about that junket were replete with some very rich invective indeed—usually the trips were held to two or three days. Good thing, too, for Mary's driving was never much and it got progressively worse. Wherever she drove, it was often in the wrong lane and at one half the going rate of speed. As a young passenger, I hated the inevitable moment in some newly arrived at place where Mary would stop to ask directions from a pedes-

Top: The jelly factory on the hill. *Above*: B&M F-2 A&B 4225 at White River Junction.

trian ("any old stumblebum" as Grandma Beth described the routine), never pulling the car sufficiently far to the right in doing this to allow the line of cars stacked up behind her, surely eight or nine vehicles by now, to get around.

As a high-strung kid, I was amazed by these actions, but I loved her sense of adventure. She would read about some gift shop in Northern Maine or a famous tearoom on a cranberry bog and we'd be off in no time.

"Your Aunt Mary's coming down to get you Friday afternoon after school," my mother jubilantly announced. Her obvious pleasure, I realize in retrospect, came in the anticipation of having one fewer child around for a couple of days. "She wants to take you to a jelly factory." Mary thus collected me, and Grandma Beth from her house in Salem, taking us off to Winchester for the night, and early Saturday morning we were off in search of the quest. Now, I use the phrase "in search of" to make it clear that Mary never bothered with formal directions, a habit which used to drive my Grandmother, and me as I grew older, to near distraction, the more so because it took years for me to catch on to this characteristic. One would sort of intuit this lack of specificity as the general area of destination was neared, and subsequent strangers queried about the quarry.

This trip, Mary had possibly read, or heard third-

Potter Place Station in the waning light of late afternoon. RWJ photo

hand, that two older ladies operated a wonderful and quaint jelly factory on the side of Mt. Monadnock. Mt. Monadnock is a pretty big hill, as I relearned years later when I bicycled over one side of its base. So we drove up through Jaffrey and Peterboro looking for what Mary was sure would be so well known to the locals that we would have no trouble at all locating it. But no one *had* heard of it, so we continued looking.

The trip was nonetheless wonderful for me. We drove through all manner of picturesque, small towns, many with delicious old train stations, and once or twice we were actually blessed with that most glorious of sights, a moving train. I have two wonderfully vivid visual memories of this day. The first was looking back over a green and gold valley in southern New Hampshire, after a long up-hill climb, its vast, magical softness touched by the late afternoon sun and a mere whisper of a breeze. The second was of an elegant, white New England inn where I was treated, for the first time, to the delights of Swedish Coffee Cake. The additional whole cake, brought forth hot from the kitchen to please *the child*, was for me a perfectly reasonable substitute for the as yet unfound jelly factory.

We returned home the next day, richer for the many glorious vistas and train stations.

Aunt Mary was also especially tenacious, so when she read about the true jelly factory in 1961, this time she saved the article which told of the location. Some eight years had passed since the first quest and poor Mary's driving had developed such idiosyncracies that my Dad no longer considered it safe for her to drive these trips with me or my Grandmother. With a little urging from me, he agreed to take us. By this time, my

real motive was that the jelly factory was situated high on a hill above Potter Place, New Hampshire, a mere 39 miles from White River Junction. This was one of those special railroad places I had dreamed about, often so far away as to be inaccessible, but which now with a little gentle persuasion might be mine.

So, one fine autumn day we were off, Dad, Mary, Beth, my brother Geoff, and me. Mom stayed home because Mary made her hysterical (and Mary's disapproval of my Mother was none too well veiled). By early afternoon we had found the place. It would take some stretch of the imagination to construe this spot as being on Mt. Monadnock. Mt. Kearsarge, maybe, some fifty miles more to the north. And indeed the jelly was made and jarred on the premises by two charming older ladies, whom we met.

Lunch eaten, jellies consumed and appreciated, a nearby horse patted, and with liberal quantities of jelly squirrelled into the car for many Sunday breakfasts to come, we set out again, this time for the more sensible fodder of Boston & Maine trains.

I am grateful to Dad and the rest of the family with us that day that I was indulged as far as I was, that we got to White River Junction at all, for I did get some nice shots. Judging from the activity around the station, the full baggage carts, the men here and there, we probably arrived just before the 4 p.m. rush when four passenger trains would converge and swap people, baggage, mail and express. Here I saw my first F unit diesel painted in the McGinnis blue scheme (4225), and I got two fine shots of the depot itself in the afternoon light. I photographed the shiny black B&M American, 494 (Manchester, 1892) on a display in a little park just across the White River in East Hartford, Vermont (in terrible shape today, I'm afraid). Had I known more, I would have pleaded to stay past four to shoot "the action." And had I known enough to ask Dad for that, I surely would have come prepared with more film. But Dad had wanted to start back, as he hated driving in the dark. As it was, we left White River Junction with one frame of film left. The light was fading as we headed Southeast toward Boston, paralleling the B&M New Hampshire Division, and I asked if I could use my last shot on the little gingerbread depot at Potter Place, which we had hastened past earlier in the day. To my dismay, when the slides were processed, I discovered that there hadn't been quite a full frame of film, thus trimming the station, but because the picture as it is has so much meaning for me, and all the memories, I have included it here anyway.

Boston

"Wutz Yawz?" she said with a poker face, the lady behind the Savarinette Counter in North Station. "A plain hamburger and a coke," I responded, having made the necessary translation of her strong Boston accent into the literal "What's Yours?," or from there what she really meant being "What will you have?" Always the same lady, always the same question. She was like an institution, eternally there when I'd go to Boston for a day of hanging around the stations, North and South, taking yet more pictures of Budd Cars, though at South Station one always had plenty of heavyweight and conventional streamlined equipment. There was a sadly faded green New York Central E-7 which creaked and

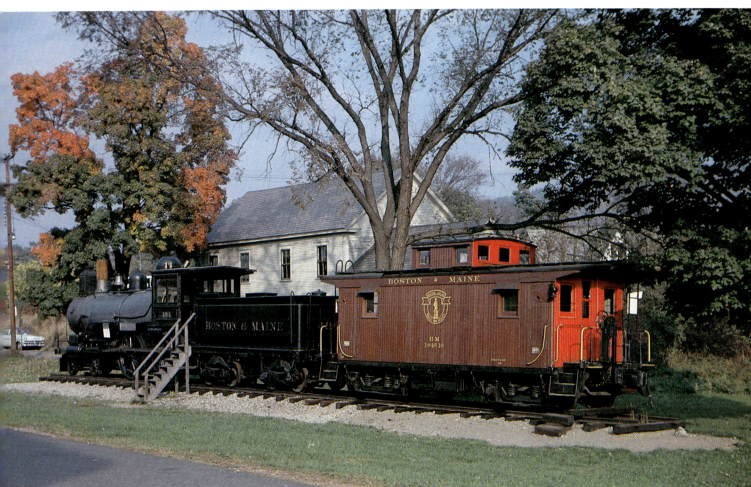

Above: B&M American 494 and a wooden caboose on display in East Hartford, Vermont in October 1961.
Top: Candy Lou Gellin at North Station. Two photos, RWJ.

crawled weekdays with a string of turtle-backed coaches between Boston and Framingham. It is said that the Smithsonian Institution tried unsuccessfully for years to get its hands on them.

But the hamburgers at the Savarinette were great. The counter was right there out in the stream of traffic where you could see everything. If you were rushing for a train and didn't have time to grab a sandwich in the station, there was always a good chance you would encounter Candy Lou Gellin either on the platform or on the train in the minutes before it left. "Peanits, choon gum, choklit bahs" he would intone loudly on his way through the car. And he did a pretty good business, too, all things considered. He even had a business card.

Sometimes I thought of the terminal as the "Incredible Shrinking North Station." Every time I went, something else would have been closed up. The fact that Mr. McGinnis turned out to be a crook (I refer to his conviction stemming from a "kick-back" on the sale of the Railroad's streamlined coaches), sometimes obscures the possible productive motives behind the seemingly Machiavellian acts. His effort to maximize returns to the stockholders on real-estate development was a perfectly reasonable idea. McGinnis knew, and

tried to tell everyone else, that private railroads should not be burdened with commuter train deficits. If our society had come to its senses twenty years earlier than it did, we would still have the four bascule bridges and 23 tracks at North Station which existed through the 1950s instead of the present two and twelve.

As a little boy I saw the big, complete North Station, where you could board the train just past the gate off the main concourse, where a roll sign was displayed for each train. In a very short time around 1959 (remember that service to Marblehead and Danvers via Wakefield Junction was eliminated that year), the tracks were reduced from 23 to 11, and in 1961 those remaining 11 shortened to about the place where the expressway bisects the terminal, with all the resulting land leased out for parking. There's no denying the tracks were redundant *then*, or that the parking revenues weren't sorely needed. It's just that it was all so short sighted.

I want to tell you about the North Station roll signs. Did you ever wonder what happened to them all? Well, so did I. So one day I made friends with Al Trunello, the day Gateman, who was a wonderfully friendly and loquacious guy. He was always, always ready to answer my questions or just to talk shop, which

On a snowy winter morning in the early 1960s we're looking into North Station from one of two remaining bascule bridges crossing the Charles River. RWJ photo.

is what I really wanted. Al showed me where the sign room was in the basement of the express building, from where he took a couple of the signs he was sure would never be used again and gave them to me. Always acquisitive, I found my appetite whetted for more. On my next visit, I queried Al about how I could meet Ted, the sign painter. "Just go there when he's there," Al encouraged, "He'll help you." Ted had many other sign painting duties on the railroad, so finding him in required persistence, but eventually I did. He was gentle, soft-spoken, very friendly, and willing to help. He gave me twelve roll signs, each made obsolete because of the myriad cutbacks of the late fifties and early sixties, most of them in perfect condition. The best was for a train to Intervale at the end of the Conway Branch, 5:30 p.m. from Boston, lettered *Mountaineer* at the top in green and white (page 106).

Ted was of the old school, a master sign painter. His signs were art. His lettering went down simply and easily. No stroke was wasted or repeated. It was perfect the first time. As train service was trimmed back on some of the lines (say, from Troy to Williamstown, then to Greenfield, on the Fitchburg Division), the stations on the bottom of the sign were painted out with black. Ted showed me how to remove the black-out so that I could see what was there originally. Then I could fill in with white over his prior work. "Go to an art store and get some Striping White in Japan. Mix that with a little clear varnish and that's your lettering medium." Imagine that, I thought, something actually called Striping White in Japan.

My collection was now fourteen roll signs. Not bad, I thought. But I want them all, my heart said. My second Gateman friend was Johnny Cronin, who had the night shift, starting at 4 p.m. Johnny was tall and thin, about 60, with a great shock of white hair. I had known him and pestered him for many months when one night during my roll-sign sickness I had an idea. "Johnny, whatever happened to the signs for Marblehead after they closed down service in '59?" "Real strange you should ask that," he said, "They're outside in the trunk of my car. D'you want 'em?" Is the reader familiar with the term "elation"? Surely I had died and gone to train heaven! It seems that one of the regular Marblehead commuters, an attorney who typically rode the last of three evening trains, had asked Johnny if he would mind holding them until he could return the following week to pick them up. "He never came back," Johnny lamented, "and I've held them for him ever since."

Seventeen signs and rolling.

For as many times as I looked for Ted again, I never found him down in the darkness of the sign room. Though I am *not* as honest as the day is long, as you will discover if you read on, I did not have the temerity to steal the sign room key from the Trainmaster's room, where it hung on the wall deliciously close to the public door. Not only was I terrified of being caught in fla-

Two of the last three roll signs in use for Marblehead service. Two photos, RWJ.

grante delicto, but more of being caught by Trainmaster Tenney himself.

After the tracks were cut back to the overhead expressway, eventually all passenger passage to and from trains was consolidated at one large gate area near the former exit door for Track 2, now six or eight doors across. This done, the roll signs were moved to this area in a single, large display case. Sometime during this transition period, I noticed that the roll sign storage bins beyond track 11 were neglected and completely ignored. I reasoned that anything I would find in them would not be needed, since the new gate area had its full contingent of signs.

Children, there is treasure at the end of the rainbow. Lost and forgotten at the bottom of the bin to Track 12 was the roll sign for the *Rockingham Racer* in beautiful shape. The large stylish lettering was done in red and cream, with a blank spot where the gateman was supposed to chalk in the departure time, since at one time the train had run in several sections. The 1958 timetable, in fact, shows Monday through Saturday departures at 12:15 p.m., with another Saturday only train departing first at 12:05 p.m. The *Rockingham Racers* were not run this year, 1962, and the word around North Station was that they would not again. My alibi for taking the sign is thus forever protected. It was surplus material. Would I have returned it had I read an announcement by the Railroad that they were starting up the train again? That really is the question. Probably not.

For awhile I would hang several roll signs on a wall here and there, rotating them from the rest of the stack under the bed, but eventually I stored them all in a box. Having them gave me enormous pleasure, perhaps that associated with the chase more than anything else. They made me feel close to trains of the B&M which I

had not and would never be able to ride. Phrases like "Sleeping car for Van Buren" fired my imagination about railroading in Northern Maine—this from a roll sign for the train formerly called the *Gull*.

In 1985, at age 39, I realized that I, too, am mortal and that I should ensure that these mementos of a great era should be placed in proper hands. I gave them to the Boston & Maine Railroad Historical Society for their archive.

Boston Engine Terminal

My pack of the Marblehead Cub Scouts took us, some 40 strong, into Boston on a Saturday afternoon to visit Boston Engine Terminal. What a grand time! I have one very vivid memory of coming out the side door of the dark roundhouse into the sunlight to see the most gorgeous bright green pair of A unit diesels in shiny new paint you could ever imagine, looking for all the world just like the ones I had seen in the Lionel Catalogue (to my undiscerning, eye, anyway). Years later it dawned on me that what I had seen must have been from the Maine Central, but for all those years I couldn't fathom why the B&M would have had green diesels (You would think I would have read the lettering!) I don't think then that I knew there *was* a Maine Central Railroad, let alone that they had green diesels (I believe the first green paint scheme on the Maine Central dates from 1953). It was on this trip that our Scoutmaster told us that Budd Cars would soon be coming to Marblehead. And there was indeed a short moment in time when our little town on the sea was served by steam, diesel, and RDCs all at once.

On one especially rainy afternoon when I went to meet Dad at the Marblehead Depot I encountered an unexpected grouping of equipment. On this day a train of Budd Cars occupied the Salem track while a steam engine had brought in a string of conventional red coaches on the main track adjacent to the Depot. The Budd Cars experienced difficulty with the excessive rain and were placed temporarily on the Salem track until the weather improved.

Thinking back to the Roundhouse at the Boston Engine Terminal, I recall one strange experience I had with George Hill, Director of Public Relations for the Boston & Maine.

F-2A 4256 in its fine blue paint scheme, undergoing maintenance at the Boston Engine Terminal. RWJ photo.

George was a master photographer and during his many years on the Railroad compiled a fine collection of material. He preferred the term "making" pictures instead of "taking" pictures, not only more accurate but much more poetic. Somehow my Dad had come to know George Hill as well as George Glacy, Vice President for Finance. (I believe it related to the Railroad's business with the Post Office Department, where Dad was Regional Real Estate Manager for New England.) Both Hill and Glacy heard from my Dad that I liked trains, and wanting to be accommodating, they told him to send me around sometime for a personal tour of the Boston Engine Terminal. Dad was a little leery of the whole idea—not wishing to be beholden to them, as he was always especially careful in his work to avoid even the appearance of impropriety—but he eventually relented and allowed me to call George Hill.

I can only describe the impetuous way I handled the visit by admitting that I still retain some embarrassment over it. I should have waited until I had some money to buy film, because the day I chose I had none. I thought something would turn up. Dad somehow knew that although I had a camera with me, I didn't have any film, and he warned me before we left the house that morning that he had almost no cash right then and that it really wasn't the best day to go. But since I had the day off from school, a very rare thing on a weekday, I was determined to proceed.

So Dad and I drove to Wonderland where we parked and rode the MTA into Boston. We both went to his office in the Federal Building on Milk Street and then I walked to North Station, about a mile away. George Hill greeted me in what I was to learn later was his usual breezy but slightly short style. He outlined where we were going to go and asked if I had brought film. Now I do not know why he asked me this. You would think that seeing a camera he would assume there was film in it, yet he asked all the same. I was so ashamed at not having any, since the point of the visit was to take pictures, that I made some excuse and said I needed to go get some, and that I would be back shortly. If he was surprised or annoyed, he didn't show it. So I walked back to Dad's office where I somehow hoped money would have become aplenty, but it was not to be so. I think Dad was annoyed that I had gotten myself into this pickle, and though I think he wanted me to have film, there wasn't anything to be done then. Back to North Station. George Hill did not ask if I had actually purchased film and I did not say. Together we drove out to the Engine Terminal. When we got to interesting shots which he pointed out, I pretended to make pictures by framing what I considered to be good compositions and triggering the shutter, knowing I would be damned in hell for such a ruse. He spent a good hour and a half showing me around the Budd Car house, the turntable and the roundhouse, the Wheel grinder, etc. He was indeed very nice to me.

Compounding the embarrassment and the shame of it was the sad truth that I had missed a of lot of very interesting pictures. I don't remember exactly how the morning ended, but I think Dad took me to a restaurant and charged the lunch. Credit cards didn't exist in the way they do today. It was enough to have your own personal account at a restaurant, but charging film at a drugstore would have been impossible. I'm sure I waited around to go home with Dad in the car, since I certainly didn't have the bus fare to go alone.

George Hill had a very striking photograph on his office wall. In it, passenger diesel 3813 is coming toward the camera with six streamline coaches and three heavyweight coaches behind. The double track roadbed is immaculate, and the scene is enhanced by a signal bridge spanning the tracks with four three-light masts, two facing each direction, and a billowing cumulus cloud. The photo also appears in the 1955 handbook "Railroading on the Boston & Maine," written and compiled by Hill. In the handbook, the photo is labelled "The *Kennebec*, eastbound at Scarborough, Maine." As I came into contact with other B&M literature, I noticed that these same clouds appeared frequently, which I did think was something of a coincidence. When I asked him about it, he freely explained that he simply liked the clouds which he photographed by themselves on one particularly beautiful New England day, and that he would sandwich in this negative when printing certain rail pictures because it made them look all the more dramatic. He also told me that he used the same photo to depict *The Flying Yankee* and *The Pine Tree Limited* whenever the mood struck him.

I had been given the impression by George Hill that special clearance was required to be around the Engine Terminal, yet I hadn't seen a sign that anyone paid us the slightest heed. And in the weeks which followed, this notion played in my head, culminating in my simply repeating the same itinerary, this time *without* the benefit of Mr. Hill or other escort but *with* film. As you might imagine, no one batted an eye. Once, railroads had tight security, but in 1961 the B&M was making reductions wherever it could, and security was not a high priority. The images of the various pieces of rolling stock and equipment in these buildings were engrossing and magnetic. It was completely unlike any other place I saw on the Railroad. My Ektachrome slides, badly color-shifted as they are with the blue almost gone, are still among my favorites.

In my listening to various Railroad people during my first few months of active interest, I would often hear references to "the third floor." This referred, I finally discerned, to the third floor of the B&M Office building at 150 Causeway Street where the Chief Dispatcher's headquarters were located. More, the B&M had begun the process of consolidating the control modules from the various signal towers, bringing them to Boston and closing the towers. The idea that such a place existed for a railroad, a veritable war room from where you could control the empire, was all that was needed to get my adrenalin going. Fearless from my mission to the Engine Terminal I determined to conquer "the third floor" alone. I walked into the lobby at 150 Causeway Street and, unchallenged by the liveried elevator boys, I went up to 3 and got off. With a little wandering it was easy enough finding the CTC boards with their illuminated track diagrams and so I took four photographs without resistance from anyone even though there were train directors manning the boards. Some weeks later I went back with actual prints to hand out to these gentlemen, simply as tokens of my interest, and perhaps a few minutes of train talk. (Before doing this, I had found someone who identified each of the operators for me so I knew the names.) The first and last that day was Bernard Smith, Train Dispatcher. In a dismissive tone, he accused me of taking the photo out of the B&M Employee Magazine, a copy of which he produced. Even though it was in black and white while mine was in color, and was obviously (to me at least) not the same shot, he persisted. He did not actually accuse me of wanting money for it, but that clearly was the implication. This was surely the moment to take my leave. I left the print anyway but he looked mighty disgusted.

Higher up in the building, on the same floor as the Passenger Traffic Department, was the Executive Suite. Stepping off the elevator, one knew instantly that this was sacred territory. While every other inch of the B&M and its plant looked used and worn, though reliable, the decor here was very snappy and au courant. The ceiling had been lowered and the lights sunken up inside, and there was a massive door painted gloss black with EXECUTIVE in large white, classic looking letters. After summoning up enough courage to pass

through, having concocted some hypothetical question for the receptionist inside, I discovered only an antiroom with an empty desk, a telephone, and instructions to call inside. I weighed the idea of going further and, though I hate confrontations, decided to press on. I went through several doors and hallways before I actually found anyone at all. I arrived at an open door to a vast office, regally furnished in a rich, dark wood with a resplendent deep emerald green carpet. Seated at the desk was a distinguished looking gentleman in a very black, correct business suit. I still don't know who it was, but I felt I had gone far enough. For, whatever hypothetical question I might have formulated, it clearly wasn't going to work here. After all, what does a fifteen year old kid say to McGinnis or George Glacy or Daniel Benson or whoever the hell it was? "Can we chat a minute about your plans for surplus real estate on the railroad?" "How much longer are you going to string the public along with your promises to keep passenger trains?" "Excuse me, did I leave my pen here?" "Where is the gang plank, please? I wish to jump." Perhaps the reader would have known what to say, but chutzpa failed me and I fled. I don't even think the man saw me.

For all the supposed excitement of the Dispatcher's area on the third floor, it wasn't ultimately so special. It was removed from the trains. That's why I much preferred the real towers, like Tower A.

Located just across the drawbridge from North Station, Tower A was the nerve center for passenger train movements between the station and the Engine Terminal, and the beginnings of their corridors to the Fitchburg Division, the New Hampshire mainline, and the Boston Division—both East and West (these were the designations during the McGinnis years; the latter two had at one time been Portland Division, East and West).

Right: Tower A in the snow in 1963. RWJ photo.

Opposite page: E-7s 3810 and 3812 awaiting disposal at the Schiavone Scrap Yard beneath the Mystic River Bridge. Norton D. Clark photo.

One winter day I went up the stairs and asked if I could look around and take a few pictures. Though I was a little apprehensive, I was very graciously received. What struck me immediately about every B&M tower I was to go into was the obsolete trackage on the track diagram; every one showed sections of track no longer needed and now removed. At Tower A, it was tracks 12 through 23 of North Station. These, representing just over half of the terminal's capacity, had been wiped out along with the removal of No. 3 and No. 4 draw-bridges, to make way for a parking lot. Worse, of the 11 remaining tracks, track one was inaccessible because it butted up against the old express building and was principally used, formerly, for head-end traffic make-up. And, the first third of each of the ten remaining working tracks was lifted for yet more parking space. It was pretty damned disgraceful, and in case there had been any doubts about Mr. McGinnis's intentions, they were clear enough now.

Trainmaster Tenney

I did get stopped once. I had been so completely unchallenged prior to this incident that it took me completely by surprise.

For a year or so in the early 1960s, the only non-Budd RDC passenger equipment (except for the Talgo Train) to grace North Station was car 4444, the former heavyweight dining car No. 87, *Massachusetts*, built in December 1930, and converted to Instruction Car 3333 in 1950 (later 4444). It occupied a spot at the end of track

two during this time until it was eventually moved out to the Engine Terminal. One Saturday Lincoln Soule and I were in North Station for the purpose of taking the train back to Salem when we spotted a Budd Car being used to move car 4444. There seemed to be an unusually large crew around. We went over for a closer look and a photo. A very fat man in a soft hat with rodent like eyes came at me, snapping "No pictures, no pictures!" As he darted toward me he grabbed his hat away from his head and held it toward me, blocking my camera lens. He then informed me that this was private property and that any picture taking was strictly at his pleasure, which it definitely was not at this moment. Because I was now the center of attention of these dozen or so employees, I retreated with my tail between my legs, not really sure why all this had transpired. Only later did I learn from a friendly trainman that my adversary had been Ray Tenney, North Station Trainmaster[5], and that moving anything with a Budd Car was a big no-no, seriously frowned upon by the Brotherhood and by the Budd Company itself. The whole incident shook me up and made me feel very guilty, but for all the times I was in North Station after that I scarcely ever saw Ray Tenney again. And I was never again stopped from taking pictures anywhere on the Railroad.

The End of the Es

One hot summer day while I was hanging around the departure gates at North Station, Al Trunello told me that the remaining E-unit passenger diesels, the

B&M's 3800s, were under the Mystic River Bridge at "Shabony's" just before being cut up for scrap (Twenty years later I actually saw the name of this scrap dealer in print, and it is "Schiavone"). So I hiked out to Mystic Wharf, about an hour's walk on the tracks, to photograph what was there. It was pretty sad. Here were the road's once proud passenger diesels, and one or two F-2s, stripped of their motors, now just brittle shells, their paint fading in the baking sun. Down at one end were some decrepit heavyweight passenger cars, which, because they were of another road (I think New Haven) I didn't bother to photograph. Sadly, I never did actually take a photo of a 3800-class diesel under power. The one time I could have was my first outing in Winchester with my new 35mm Baldessa. I missed getting 3809, the last active E-unit on the B&M, on the point of a White River Junction milk train, and several other glorious shots, because I had left the lens cap on. At least I was fortunate to find 3809 in the engine house in Boston one day, where I got a nice interior shot of her. Also at Schiavone's was 3814, the only E to receive the McGinnis paint scheme, and in my opinion, the best application of that design. (This was the diesel donated by the B&M to Pleasure Island for display, but the amusement park failed and it was returned to the railroad. Had there been a need for them, and had proper maintenance been applied, these diesels could have had 20-plus year lives instead of the 11 to 16 they served. Only 3821 survived, an E-8 purchased in 1950. It was sold to the Missouri Pacific in 1962 for passenger service where it lasted until 1972 when it was traded in to EMD.)

This was the Boston I knew: a shadow of the complex rail center it once had been, but still full of wonderful things like a poignant image of the last night train out of North Station, the 12:10 a.m. single Budd for Rockport. Moments like this on the B&M had an intimacy and a sadness that were quite special.

Without the camera

Collecting my vision of the B&M meant that occasionally I took a trip without the camera (a stupid idea in retrospect!). I recall one gorgeous sunny spring day when I rode up to Newburyport and back just for the ride. The Brakeman told me the story of the Appleton Farm in Ipswich which extended for many acres on either side of the B&M right of way. In return for an easement through the property, the farm's owners were granted rights, in perpetuity, to flag any Eastern Railroad train (the B&M's predecessor on this line) and take free passage. As he understood the arrangement, the agreement was still in effect, though unused. With that day's terrific scenery and that fine weather, I comtemplate wistfully what wonderful pictures there might have been.

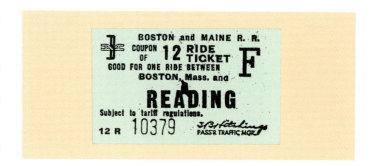

Reading

A rush-hour trip to Reading in an eight-car Budd Train was just the thing, I thought, for a spiced-up late afternoon of visiting North Station. A short trip such as this was ideal for me because I could do it after school and still be home for dinner. By contrast, if I wanted to go to Portsmouth, I wouldn't be able to return until the following morning since there were no incoming trains after the hour when I could arrive there if I went after school; I can't imagine now why it didn't occur to me to go on Saturday or Sunday.

The only way to ride in a cab, short of going through George Hill in the Public Relations Office (and that meant both signing a release and buying a ticket, a cumbersome and expensive process), was to ask the particular engineer. One's chances for success were about 75 percent. This day I encountered a very friendly engineer and fireman. The route was of special significance to me, because this is where the *Flying Yankee, Pine Tree Limited, Kennebec,* and the *Gull* all traveled. This was the once famous Portland Division West, its passenger service now comprised of some very substantial commuter business. Because of the McGinnis plan to use the *Wildcat*[6] beyond Wilmington Junction on the New Hampshire Division, trains to North Conway and Portland now went north via that route rather than through Reading.

My strongest memory of the trip is of kids playing on the tracks, coming into vision as we rounded one curve at 70 mph. The engineer lay on the horn and they scattered instantly, but you could see the fear in his face. With eight Budd Cars behind us, it would have been another half mile before we could have stopped. Riding in a cab gives one a very clear picture of just how vulnerable moving trains are to these dangers. You think, "That Budd Car which hit the oil truck in Everett late one night, surely he could have stopped." After a cab ride in a fast train, you'll never think that again.

We were in Reading just long enough for the three of us to walk through the train, do an air test, and highball express to Boston, where the same crew then returned with the equipment to Reading for another run and back. As we pulled into North Station there must have been three hundred people already on the platform. In ten minutes the train was off again.

Noon Salem Meets

The McGinnis operations people produced one innovation of special note with respect to operations at Salem. Early on in the coming of the Budd Cars the railroads got a concession from the unions that a single Budd Car could operate with only an engineer at the head end (Since an RDC weighed 44 tons, it fell below the 45 ton limit, after which a fireman was mandated) The addition of another or multiple cars would thus require the presence of a fireman. The B&M took advantage of the plan in the following manner. A two-car Budd train traveled from Boston to Salem with both an engineer and a fireman. At Salem the two cars were separated by the Car Knocker, one of the cars then going up the Gloucester Branch, the other to Newburyport or Portsmouth. The engineer took one and the other was piloted by the engineer of one of two inbound single cars from Rockport and Portsmouth. The fireman returned to Boston on the just-formed two car train. When the two single-car trains returned to Salem from the north, the process was reversed. By the time I came on the scene, the occurence of this procedure was limited to a single daily train arriving in Salem at about 12:30 P.M. It was, nonetheless, always interesting to watch. The inbound combining of the two Budds—whereby two trains were required to enter the same block—necessitated the use of a signal device known as a "call on" signal, activated by the train director at Salem Tower. It produced a flashing yellow indication on the lowest of three lights on the home signal adjacent to Salem Tower. The message was clear to the engineer: The block is occupied, but you have business there so proceed slowly and cautiously.

The Car Knocker was a colorful character. "Earthy" might be more accurate. He was a committed cigar chomping type with skin the consistency of a work ox, nut brown from years in the sun. He spent all day outdoors. The Salem freight office was a little wooden tower affair and one day when I was hanging around, absorbing the ever-present smell of a local tannery's leather discards rotting in gondolas, I came across this fellow sitting on the wooden bench just in front of the tower. He was rather stout, and short too, and it was this day I learned about his unusual habit of pulling his pants down when he sat down to relax so that his blue jeans (now a filthy gray-brown) wouldn't bind on him. Because his shirt hung around his very ample belly as he sat, I didn't see any of this until he stood up. The wardrobe did not include underwear. In retrospect I don't know why I should have been embarrassed since he clearly wasn't. Ah, life on the railroad.

There was the usual vandalism now and again, most of it in the category of annoyance rather than anything very serious. The local B&M policeman, Julius Wasserstram, encountered me one day taking pictures, and was perfectly nice about my being on the property. I think Burr Town at the tower had put in a good word

The Salem Car Knocker separates two Budd RDCs during the daily noon-time procedure, as a father and his boy watch from the opposite track. RWJ photo.

anyway, so the way was paved. Julius did suggest once that I should photograph anyone I saw doing anything wrong. Dad became apoplectic when he heard about this. "Great! The guy's trying to get you killed. Just great! Don't you ever go anywhere near any vandals with your camera!"

Secretly, I planned to cooperate with Julius, but I never saw anyone do anything bad. In fact, I rarely saw anybody doing anything around the B&M. Wherever I went I mostly had train watching to myself. I can't recall ever actually seeing anyone taking a photo of the railroad. Twice in South Station I met a guy named Paul, about my age, who watched trains. Once he had an ice cream cone and the other time he had a camera. But never on the B&M.

REMEMBERING THE SIGNAL MAINTAINER

"Y ou have so many questions," Bill Sveda interjected, "we could spend a whole day together." Bill Sveda was the B&M's signal maintainer for all the Eastern Route territory north of Pickman Park in Salem. That is, the mainline as far north as Ipswich, the Gloucester Branch, the Peabody-Danvers-Topsfield Branch, so altogether he had a lot of ground to cover. His responsibilities were extensive. He was expected to keep in order—and did so—all the railroad signalling mechanisms, beginning with the actual track signals to the hundreds of relays which activated them in Salem Tower and at each location, down to the myriad grade crossing signals depended upon to protect the public.

After his evaluatory statement about how long it would take to answer my questions, he suggested that perhaps I would like to spend a day with him observing him at work.

Bill Sveda on the job, somewhere on the North Shore, at a very unusual crossing signal. RWJ photo.

This was especially exciting to me, because I did indeed have a burning fascination for signals and how they worked.

We met at the Salem Enginehouse, the once active roundhouse, where much of his raw material was stored. It was from this shop that he would keep his special truck stocked, a vehicle which at any time held thousands of the many parts which might be needed for a quick repair of some very vital signal. It was Bill Sveda who paternally explained to me how signals work, how a low-amperage electrical current is at all times flowing through the rails. This current, when a train is present, flows through the wheels and axle of the train to complete an electrical circuit which triggers track signals, crossing gates, etc.

We visited many spots that day where Bill went up one crossing signal to replace a burned out bulb, put in new signal bonds (those heavy wires spanning the gap between two rails to ensure a good electrical connection), and we even ventured onto Beverly drawbridge where I was fascinated to find a set of vintage Armstrong levers. These lowered the gates to block the path of an approaching train when the bridge was open. Both the highway drawbridge and the rail bridge at Beverly were rotating bridges, both controlled by the same operator. Much to my delight, Bill worked the levers so I could get pictures.

He showed me the huge, powerful, and expensive lenses which enable a target signal to send off the arresting bright light down the track straight into the eyes of the engineer. This is possible, of course, only on a railroad and not on a highway, because the train's route is always unchanged.

We looked into grade crossing relay boxes where Bill made routine maintenance replacement of certain components. He had a schedule set up so that he handled a few such different boxes each day, and he got to everything every six months.

What really stands out from that day is Bill's invitation to his home for lunch, where his wife made a superb Polish vegetable bean soup. The memory of that wonderful taste is with me still, as is the thoughtful and generous spirit of the gesture. He was a genuinely kind man, and surely among the most professional and conscientious of B&M employees.

Former Signal Maintainer David Lamson describes how Bill Sveda was perceived by his colleagues:

Bill had the reputation of being a gentleman. He would work with you and not against you, would teach you without demeaning you, and would advise without undermining your authority. Jimmy Martin, my mentor (an excellent case man turned signal maintainer), named Bill as one of our best signal personnel, being the most professional person to work with, the most knowledgeable to learn from, and—perhaps most important—the nicest person to associate with.

Tickets

Morale got low sometimes in the face of McGinnis's trimming of the payroll. Nonetheless, one particular fellow in the ticket office was always happy and courteous. "I'd like a parlor car seat to Winchester," I bandied. "Would you like the sunny side of the car?" he retorted with a grin.

To Andover and Lawrence

In our family blood is the urge to roam, to drop everything of the moment to go in search of adventure. My Aunt Mary had a bad case, but mine was worse. One summer night I biked down to Lincoln Soule's house on Front Street in Marblehead. Only his Father, Floyd, was home. "Ruth's taken Lincoln and Alexis camping up in a park in South Andover. I took them up yesterday in the trailer and they'll be there a week. Why don't you bike up there and join them?" Now, *here* was a challenge. I got my Mother to say yes, and off I went for a two-hour bike ride to the camp. It was a lovely and idyllic spot up a little hill from a beautiful pond, first created in the 1930s by the Civilian Conservation Corps. In the morning the water in the pond was so still that it looked like glass. The camp's distance north of Marblehead gave us new possibilities in train watching. So after one day of swimming and hiking around the camp, and looking for new diversions, we took off for Andover, a bike ride of some 45 minutes, where we were rewarded with an appearance of M2, the Mechanicville-Portland freight, heading east at Andover Station. That done, we took to the road for the Lawrence depot, a crisp looking building, where I got good station shots but no train. On the way back we saw a roundhouse, which I photographed, miserably out of focus, and a gravel train from far, far, off so that photo was also a disaster. Fortunately it was a wonderfully sunny day, a valued commodity. Sadly, deep gray skies followed the next day when we travelled west 18 miles to Wilmington Junction, where the New Hampshire Division splits off to the left and the *Wildcat* heads to the right. We did manage to get a shot of a local freight heading southbound past a green-over-green distant signal. The station itself had the unusual feature of a strangely high order board, so built to be seen by northbound trains *over* the highway bridge adjacent to the depot. Our trip back was to be a long one, the afternoon light was getting darker and darker under threatening skies, and we didn't know whether there would be any more moments of trains which would be photographable in the low light.

There really is a beautiful camaraderie in these trips with a friend, the sharing of physical exertion on a bike, getting winded on hills. The sheer and absolute gloriousness of going down a steep hill so fast you're scared you'll "wipe out."

A local freight crosses over to the southbound main as it leaves Wilmington for Boston in August 1961. The distant signal shows green over green. RWJ photo.

The Mighty Fitchburg

It was the route of the *Minute Man*, and it was my dream to explore it. Alas, I was only ever able to savor a handful of isolated locations on the Fitchburg.

Now forgotten is my family's destination one day when we crossed Massachusetts on the Mohawk Trail and high up by the Hairpin Turn I put a dime into a telescope and gazed down on the twisting B&M double track mainline. No trains there, just the shimmering air rising up off the heated rails on a languid summer day. Later, in 1962, when Charles Munch conducted his retirement concert from the Boston Symphony at Tanglewood to close the season of the Berkshire Music Festival, I convinced my friend Sally Bryne, who was older and had a car, that we should make a weekend of it. During the trip out on a sultry August Saturday, we had stopped at Erving to photograph the old wooden station when shortly we heard the whine of approaching diesels.

I braced myself for a swiftly passing train—I had my 116 bellows camera and there would be just one shot. I braced myself some more. And more. But the train was slowing rapidly, and as it came around the bend it was obvious it would stop. Four "Bluebirds" were leading a Portland-bound freight. As one can see from the photograph below, the crew had a meeting at the front of the train. Five minutes later they were again underway to the east, the little station at Erving seeming as deserted as before.

The next day I convinced Sally we should stop down at Lenox Station, located some two miles from the village in a pastoral setting called Lenoxdale, to catch the New Haven's New York-Pittsfield train. Powered by two FL-9s led by No. 2016, the consist included two "American Flyer" and two clerestory coaches and a New Haven heavyweight baggage car at the rear. Then later, on our way homeward following the concert, Sally stopped again at a highway crossing in Northampton so I could photograph the passenger station and nearby industrial buildings from the vantage point of one long block north.

Left: An eastbound freight pauses for crew activity at Erving, Massachusetts, 91 miles from Boston. The author's friend (and driver for the weekend) Sally Bryne, is at the right in red.

Above: In the warmth and quiet of a late afternoon in August 1962, Northampton depot hardly looks used at all. Two photos, RWJ.

This weekend trip to the Berkshires had heightened my interest and tickled my senses for the B&M's singularly beautiful Massachusetts mainline, teasing my imagination as to what it must have been like riding the parlor observation of the *Minute Man* in the 1920s on a fresh, crisp autumn day in the Berkshires, sipping apple cider, meeting new friends amidst the splendor of plush chairs and richly appointed wood paneling. If this is just one of those crazy railfan fantasies, it indeed embraces the spirit keeping my great fondness for the B&M alive all these years, containing that elusive spark enabling me to write about boyhood explorations.

I have told about the B&M I knew, yet still there was a vast complexity of railroad there—a crazy amalgam of many smaller, earlier systems—which I never saw. It was a driving passion to see what it was really like that has caused me to find those people who *were* there to capture its images on film and to inveigle them into sharing their wonderful photography with the rest of us.

Uppermost in my intentions was to find very fine photography celebrating the splendor and infinite variety of the New England countryside and cityscape. I sought colorful pictures with mighty steam engines and sleek diesels. I sought varied freight tonnage and passenger trains both luxurious and utilitarian. And whenever I could find them, I have chosen photographs with people. I wanted to have alive pictures. I wanted to show that people are at the center of the railroad's existence.

So, my friends, let us remember with fondness and pleasure that the B&M was a living thing in our world, that it never stopped changing and evolving, and that watching it during post-war years was a special priviledge for those who were there and cared to take an interest.

We cannot say that things were perfect, or even that they were better then than now. Longing for the "good old days" is a tempting pleasure of maturing in our world, a reasonable human activity, and should its yield be only that of pleasure, that is no bad thing.

We can say that the B&M was a fine railroad in a beautiful part of America, bustling to the hum of daily commerce, serving people in their livelihoods. It was a flourishing business that grew from the needs of its era. We can surely enjoy it for this.

Above: The year is 1948 and there are nine steam engines and nary a diesel in sight in this late afternnoon look at North Station. Leon Onofri photo. **Below**: Just a few years later the Expressway has imposed itself onto North Station, and while steam is not in evidence, a gas-electric car enroute to Clinton is relic enough to suit our fancy. Arthur E. Mitchell photo.

II

THE HEAD END

North Station and the Boston Engine Terminal

North Station—everyone in New England knew it. Second nature. It was just there. The 1928 structure was far more functional than pretty, a hard Yankee, no-nonsense building, having no truck with Greek revival, neo Gothic, antebellum, or any other architectural conceits. It wasn't that North Station's simple design was unsightly or ugly. On the contrary, it was actually rather dignified. But obscured by the MTA to Lechmere, coupled with the narrowness of Causeway Street, on which it fronted, the station really had no approach view. The broad sweep which one could experience at the more majestic South Station just wasn't possible here.

Even as the automobile proliferated like a family of wild rabbits, people continued to commute to Boston on the train rather than to drive. As cars supplanted trains in other endeavors—week-end driving, trips to the store, vacations, work places where the train didn't go—rail patronage went down in the countryside and held up in the city. That is, until the expressways were built.

But North Station wasn't just for commuters. Upstairs, above the concourse, grew the massive Boston Garden, home of hockey and basketball as well as the beloved circus and Ice Capades. Late-night trains carried droves of revelers home from the shows here and the plays and concerts across town. Then too, there were the daily shoppers who haunted Jordan's and Filene's and Raymond's and R. H. White's and Stearn's. With all these riders, North Station was a busy place. And everybody went there for something.

Trains were a natural part of life, it seems. And the reason was that it was simply faster and more comfortable to take the train into "town." The MTA connections at North Station were excellent. Before the Mystic Bridge opened, getting into Boston from the North was

clumsy. Before the expressways, or the improved Route 1, travel by auto into Boston was not one's favorite idea.

To handle the rail traffic, the Boston & Maine maintained a 23-track terminal at North Station, the tracks crossing the Charles River in a throat of four bascule bridges each carrying a pair of tracks. The number was no accident. With four major divisions entering Boston—Portland East, Portland West, New Hampshire, and Fitchburg—the B&M could cover four simultaneous departures and four arrivals of these divisions at once. In practice, there were more than twice as many movements as this, because equipment had to be backed in and out of the terminal before and after each run. There were no run-around tracks so an incoming engine was trapped until it backed its equipment (or until its cars were moved by a switcher into the yard for servicing). Many times the road locomotive was added to a trainset after the cars were placed in the terminal by a switcher. Also, head end cars were moved from the express track, track 1, by a switcher, for mainline trains.

An intricate labyrinth of ramps had been engineered between platform level and the second floor of the station to facilitate the movement of the express mules and their wagons, carrying baggage, mail, and Railway Express shipments between trains and the express building on the east side of the terminal.

Several things happened which obviated the need for such a large terminal. Mainline passenger traffic on the B&M went into a decline after the war and when, in the late fifties, the Post Office cancelled the mail contracts, the business all but disappeared. The once highly lucrative Railway Express business fell victim to trucking, in no small part because there were fewer and fewer trains to carry goods. Passenger service to Maine, once the fair haired boy of the line, wasted away with the completion of the Maine Turnpike. As Budd RDCs replaced more conventional equipment, there was no more need to turn trains. The whole infrastructure dedicated to the servicing of passenger equipment—switchers, yard space, maintenance facilities, huge cleaning crew, dining car commissary, Pullman car servicing—vanished in a trice.

After Patrick McGinnis assumed the presidency of the road in 1956, the maintenance budget was significantly reduced. Trains were often dirty, inside and out. Land at North Station, seen as a huge potential source of cash, was sold for parking lots. Twenty three tracks became 11, each half as long. 75% of the trackage was out of service by 1960. Two bascule bridges were removed, four throat tracks servicing what was left. A giant had been brought to his knees, bleeding profusely, mortally wounded.

For a time in history, though, North Station was a place of import in almost every local citizen's life. It was efficient and reliable. It mayn't have had much romance. But it had nobility.

Above: A close look at one piece of B&M stainless steel, mainline passenger stock—Restaurant Lounge No. 70, the Bald Eagle. Arthur E. Mitchell photo. *Below*: Mr. Mitchell was also on hand on a fine day in 1952 to ride this steam excursion to Waterville, Maine (Maine Central 467 would take over at Portland). Thoughtfully, he photographed the name board as well. Like its sister P-4 Pacifics, the 3712 was named in a competition for school children.

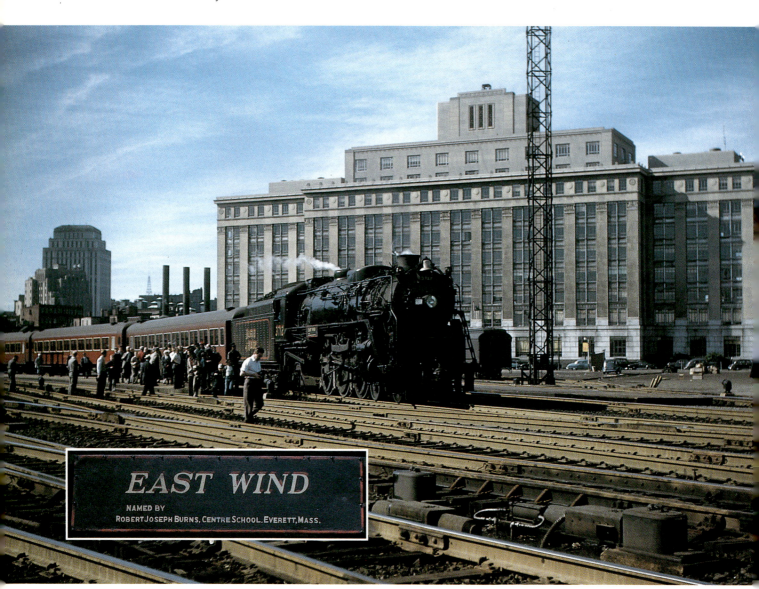

EAST WIND
NAMED BY
ROBERT JOSEPH BURNS, CENTRE SCHOOL. EVERETT, MASS.

Donald G. Hills spent a productive afternoon at North Station in June 1947, photographing whatever he could. **Above**: We have the Pine Tree Limited for Bangor, demonstrating one reason why the "Rock Island" paint scheme did not last on the 3800 diesels. Because of the frequent insertion of old, assorted head-end cars, the design did not carry directly into the new stainless coaches. Interestingly, the diesel is brown-red while the coach stripes are much brighter; the subsequent diesel scheme matched the coaches. Also, the rear of the diesel is clearly not silver, as some have asserted, but white. **Below**: Local train No. 313, the Cannonball, is about to leave for White River Junction. Both trains are slated to depart at 4:30 p.m. Note the green coach at left, a rarity by this time. Contrary to legend, the lettering is below the windows.

We have Arthur E. Mitchell to thank for these four interesting pictures of the North Station area. **Upper left**: an afternoon local passes three vintage wooden cars on its way into North Station. Prison Point Bridge is in the background. **Lower left** is an early morning, snow-dusted, bird's-eye scene from the 17th floor of the Hotel Manger, overlooking the station's 23 tracks. The long train to the left is a "Round the Mountains" excursion, and the long train toward the right is the regular Sunday morning mail and passenger train to Portland, circa 1953. **Above**: a late afternoon commuter with a healthy plume of steam heads for the Central Mass branch. **Below**: a tugboat passes below the four raised bascule bridges with Tower A in the background. Note how the fourth bridge to the right is already being lowered. Stuck bridges occasionally caused nasty delays at North Station.

North Station had a very different look by the time these two photographs were made in August 1964. **Above**: The terminal has only 11 tracks—some 100 RDCs and the Talgo Train comprising the passenger roster—and a lot of weeds. Russell F. Munroe photo.

Below: The new Expressway became a convenient point at which the McGinnis administration could truncate the station tracks—some six cars worth each—and use the land for parking. Richard W. Symmes made this sensitive rush hour shot.

For the observant B&M passenger arriving in Boston, the last mile or so before North Station was filled with a profusion of railroad rolling stock, equipment, workers, bridges, yards, freight houses, and all manner of mechanical things that spoke of railroad. Incoming trains slowed to a snail's pace while approaching the station, all the while carefully stepping through the maze of iron impedimentia, whereas their outgoing brothers always seemed to be making better progress. It was almost as if inbound engineers were taking no chances about hitting one of the bunters at the station, and so therefore they crept all the way.

Such deliberate progress through the yards made it easy to fix one's gaze on whatever railroad item caught one's fancy at that moment. There was a lot to see, and the slowed tempo of the train made it possible to take in much more than when speeding along the mainline.

The heart of this wonderful rail smorgasbord was the Boston Engine Terminal, a hub of service buildings located, literally, right in the midst of the B&M's sprawling yard action. The most imposing structure was the 50-track roundhouse, built in 1929 to service the road's considerable steam power, its turntable handling some 800 daily moves in the early 1950s. The roundhouse

could handle a major overhaul of a steam locomotive, though heavy duty jobs like the renewing of flues were done at Billerica Shop. Each steam engine was brought to the roundhouse after each run, where it would be checked, have its coal, water, and sand refilled, and the clinkers dumped from the firebox. A "turn-around" (or "nothing wrong") inspection took 20 to 35 minutes.

As diesel power was muscling out steam with a breathtaking swiftness, the roundhouse was servicing a total of 150 steam and diesel locomotives every 24 hours. Just to its west, a new diesel house was built in the late forties specifically to minister to diesel power; a complete diesel inspection was undertaken every 24 hours, some 90 locomotives every day, involving the checking of 72 individual items. In the early fifties, the B&M invested $1.5 million in another dedicated facility, this one for the burgeoning roster of Budd Rail Diesel cars (109 were eventually purchased). This efficient, 720-foot long building, located hard by the mainline, was handling 137 cars per day by 1958.

For five years in the early 1950s, Boston Engine Terminal serviced steam, diesels (including the unique Unit 6000), gas electric cars, and Budd RDCs. Surely Heaven must be like this.

One of the beloved moguls, 1493, at Cambridge for servicing on December 28, 1955 (Compare this with another photo of the same locomotive on the next page). Stephen R. Payne photo/Norton D. Clark collection.

Above left: *From a priviledged spot on the turntable, we have this interesting view of the engine terminal facility, including a string of steam switchers on the right tied up for the weekend.* **Below left**: *Mogul 1493—seen here at the roundhouse—now sports a snow-plow to keep those branch lines clear. Both photos, Arthur E. Mitchell.*

Above: *B&M 44-tonner No. 119 maneuvers 4268 B at the round-house, April 13, 1968. John F. Kane photo.* **Below**: *3821, the last-ordered of the B&M's passenger diesels, and the road's only E-8, in repose in the roundhouse. Herman Shaner photo/J. Emmons Lancaster collection.*

This page features three of Arthur E. Mitchell's fine equipment shots.

Above left: RS-3 1510 in new paint, silver trucks and white flag, proudly awaiting a run.

Center left: B&M wooden caboose 104607.

Below left: Just to show how great a shiny black Pacific can look when spanking clean, we feature B&M 3630 at the engine terminal.

Above right: Pacific 3717, Old North Bridge, gets a sharp steam cleaning as the yard hogger looks on. Leon Onofri photo/Norton D. Clark collection.

Below right: The engine terminal of October 1972 displayed many more blue and silver faces than in the past eras of black steamers and freshly painted maroon and gold diesels. John F. Kane photo.

Above left: Now here is a bracing view which not many have seen or would be likely to remember. The British flag S S Nova Scotia—in regular fortnightly service between Boston and Liverpool, England via the Canadian Maritime Provinces—makes a scheduled call at Hoosac Pier No. 1, Charlestown. The Mystic Terminal Company (Boston & Maine's foreign commerce subsidiary) had its offices in the head house of this pier leased from the Port of Boston Commission. The photograph from the Charlestown High Bridge was made on September 9, 1955 by Peter D. Victory.

Below left: Freshly painted Es—3814 and 3806—with their smart silver trucks and white flags bring to mind the moniker "high-stepping." And indeed they should be, for this is General Dwight D. Eisenhower's campaign train to Boston on October 20, 1952. The train of New York Central Pullmans was routed via Worcester, Ayer, Lowell, Lowell Junction and Reading, and for the record the engineer was F. A. Sanborn and the conductor W. R. Davis. Donald G. Hills made this shot from Tower C where he was an operator.

Above: B&M SW-9 1222 heads out to Reading and Salem with the "High Car" (so called because it circumnavigated Salem Tunnel) local on a bleak February day in 1953. Wrecking equipment is at the left; Boston Engine Terminal is in the background. Below: B&M 0-8-0 switcher 650 chuffs through Yard 7 in East Cambridge in June 1947. The Class H loco was built in 1929. Two photos, Donald G. Hills.

Two important points where the Eastern Route is touched by the sea. **Above**: *At Beverly Drawbridge, over the blue-black waters of the Danvers River, a five-car Budd RDC commuter train is bound for Boston on April 26, 1961. Allan W. Styffe photo.* **Below**: *Train C10 heads up the Piscataqua River for Newington, New Hampshire in November 1968. In the distance are the under-construction piers for the new Portsmouth-Kittery I-95 bridge. H. Bentley Crouch photo.*

III

BY THE SEA
The Eastern Route of the Portland Division

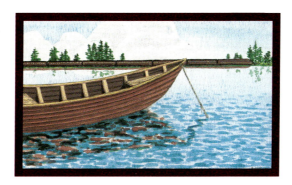

A hot sun broke blistering through the early mist to set fire to the shining grasshopper vane on Faneuil Hall, and pick out the copper-green State House dome on Beacon Hill. Long before noon the swarming North End was sweltering. The dog days had come. Urchins in the North End turned on the hydrants, while their elders tried to find relief on the steps and fire escapes of tenements. Quincy Market swarmed with flies.

Clerks in the sedate banking houses and offices of State Street were permitted to remove their jackets. Their betters merely unbuttoned the broadcloth swallowtails and Prince Alberts of their caste. After all, late afternoon or early evening would find the Hub's men of affairs in the cars of the Eastern, heading for their summer cottages and the welcome salt breezes of the North Shore.

Stewart H. Holbrook
"The Great Rail Wreck at Revere"
American Heritage

Among New England's most picturesque places are its seaside communities. The ports at Salem, Newburyport, and Portsmouth—and the interchange of goods between ships and railroads they could naturally bring—along with other towns along the route, were places people wanted to go. That train travel could get them there far more quickly and comfortably than any prior conveyance was the great public allure of the railroad boom.

Serving many of these locations in Massachusetts and New Hampshire was the Eastern Route of the Portland Division. This trackage was built by the Eastern Railroad between April 1836—the date of the first charter, and November 1840—when the first trains began running between East Boston and Portsmouth. For the next 14 years, passengers had to travel by ferry to reach Boston proper, until 1854 when the Eastern began operating on new trackage into its new depot on Causeway Street—the future sight of the 1928 North Station.

Between 1842—when the Eastern built to Maine to connect with the Portland, Saco & Portsmouth (which it controlled jointly with the B&M until 1871), so that it could operate through trains to Portland, and 1944—when war-time constraints dictated prudent economies, there were two completely separate mainlines into Maine from Boston. The first one built was the first to be truncated. All service between Kittery and North Berwick was finally concluded in September 1952, the last through passenger train having used this route one year earlier.

The B&M Eastern Route came within a hairsbreadth of becoming *the* important mainline to Portland. While the New Haven Railroad controlled the Boston & Maine between 1907 and 1914, its President, Charles S. Mellon, planned a major upgrading of the route to four tracks, with electrification as far as Beverly. Thus the 1914 grade separation project at Lynn included the four tracks for approximately a mile. Also envisioned were a tunnel under Boston Harbor from South Station to take trains onto the roadbed of the to-be-supplanted Boston, Revere Beach & Lynn, and a major relocation around Salem to bypass its single-track tunnel. But Mellon incurred the ire of the public, New

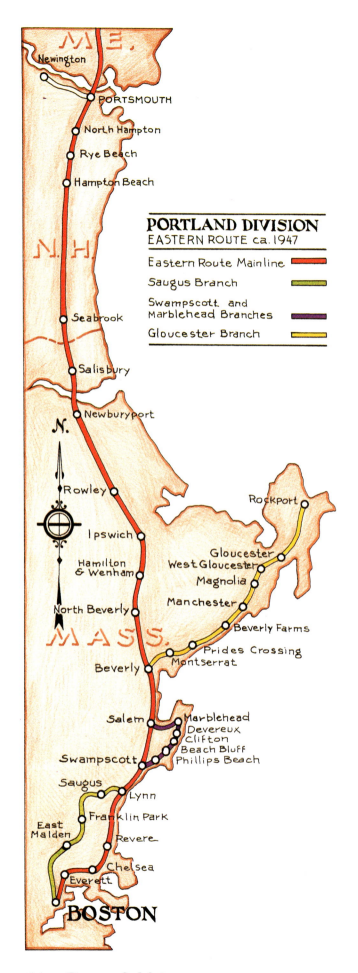

Haven control succumbed to anti-trust litigation, and the plan was abandoned.

Traffic congestion at Salem resulting from several grade crossings had become quite bad after World War I and continued to grow worse. Serious efforts in the 1930s to build a new, longer tunnel were sidetracked by World War II, and it wasn't until August 1949 that work began on the first of three phases. Two were done by the end of 1951, with a respite from construction until October 1954, when the last and most difficult commenced. Four tedious, agonizingly slow years of painful construction gripped Salem and its business district until finally, on July 31, 1958, the new tunnel opened.

As planned, the new configuration completely eliminated the former traffic congestion resulting from grade crossings, but there were losses as well. The magnificent granite depot of Norman design was reduced to just so much rip-rap for the North River dike. Far worse, the business district never recovered. The Northshore Shopping Center opened in Peabody during the tunnel's construction, considered a Godsend at the time by a public long weary of pile drivers and barricades. The remote location and nasty, steep stairways of the new station further discouraged shoppers who had used the train to come from nearby towns to shop in Salem.

Passenger service on the Eastern Route has always been frequent. As rapid transit and other public transportation proliferated around Boston, though, the seven local stops in the 11 1/2 miles to Lynn were gradually phased out. The one remaining train covering all these stops, No. 245 at 5:05 p.m. to Lynn, was gone by 1951, and the June 29, 1958 timetable eliminated East Somerville and its one morning-evening stop.

Budd RDCs first appeared on the Portsmouth timetable in 1953, with four weekday round-trips. Train No. 237 ran express the 46.5 miles to Hampton, New Hampshire in 58 minutes, 19 minutes faster than the locals.

Ridership declined through the fifties and sixties—in 1962 there were only six weekday Portsmouth trains while in 1950 there had been ten. Similarly, 1950 saw 15 trains to the Gloucester Branch (which uses the Eastern Route as far as Beverly Junction) whereas by 1962 there were only 11. The Mass Transportation Commission of the Commonwealth of Massachusetts conducted a $4 million demonstration project for 15 months in 1963-64 wherein frequency of service was increased and fares were lowered to see if ridership could be boosted.

The results were dramatic, and the eventual outcome was the formation of the Massachusetts Bay Transportation Authority, which would ultimately take control of all commuter rail service to Boston.

The only name trains to run over the Eastern Route after World War II were a pair of commuter trains called *Portsmouth Up*—outbound at 4:55 p.m., and *Portsmouth Down*—inbound at 7:20 a.m. Immediately

Above left: B&M Consolidation 2720 passes through Chelsea with a freight in August 1952. Stanley W. Cook photo. **Above right**: An aging wooden coach, one of just a handful left, finishes out its time in work service. Both it and the Salem roundhouse look forlorn and sad this December 1964 day. Richard W. Symmes photo. **Below**: Russell F. Munroe hiked out onto the mainline between Salem and Swampscott to capture this shot of an RS-3 pulling freight in July 1964.

B&M Consolidation 2725 has backed out of Salem Yard and is now onto the mainline for a trip north through the tunnel. Photographed from the Castle Hill Bridge by Russell F. Munroe.

	Rockport	Hamilton-Wenham	Newburyport	Portsmouth
Number of Round Trips in 1950, 1962, and 1963:				
1950	15	1	-	10
1962	11	1	3	6
1963*	20	2	11	6

*MTC Study

after the war they ran express to Hamilton-Wenham, making local stops thereafter. Stops at Lynn, Salem, United Shoe, and North Beverly were added gradually, supplementing the running time by 15 minutes to one hour, 38 minutes. Budd RDCs covered the schedule after 1955; Lynn and United Shoe were dropped; running time reduced to one hour, 22. The names were dropped in 1955.

Freight service was modest but profitable. The

Freight Train Symbol Book of October 31, 1954 lists the following scheduled activity:

From	To	Leave
1. Boston	Chelsea-Lynn-Salem and return via main line or Saugus Branch, makes two trips from Boston (except Sunday)	6:50 a.m.
2. Boston	Lynn via Saugus Branch and return (except Sunday)	10:00 a.m.
3. Boston	Rockport and return Work Marblehead & Topsfield (except Saturday)	7:00 p.m.
4. Salem	Amesbury and return (except Sunday)	6:35 a.m.
5. Portsmouth	Boston (except Sunday)	7:45 p.m.
6. Boston	Newington & return to Portsmouth	3:15 a.m.

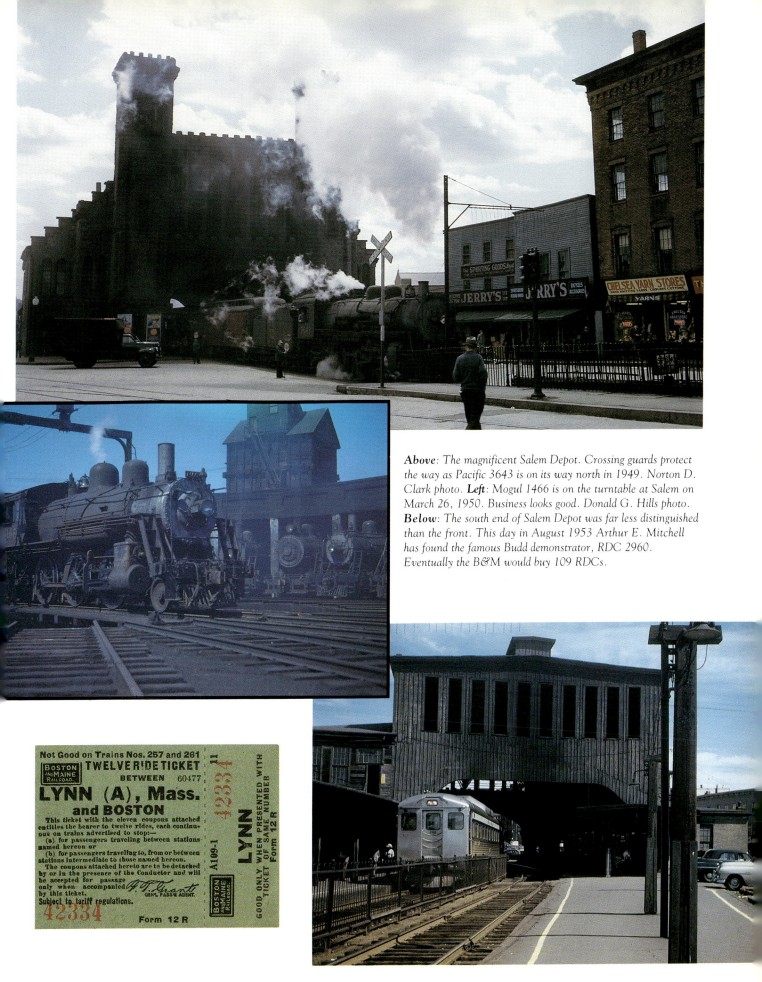

Above: *The magnificent Salem Depot. Crossing guards protect the way as Pacific 3643 is on its way north in 1949. Norton D. Clark photo.* **Left**: *Mogul 1466 is on the turntable at Salem on March 26, 1950. Business looks good. Donald G. Hills photo.* **Below**: *The south end of Salem Depot was far less distinguished than the front. This day in August 1953 Arthur E. Mitchell has found the famous Budd demonstrator, RDC 2960. Eventually the B&M would buy 109 RDCs.*

By the time of the April 1962 Symbol Book, reduced business had resulted in service cut backs. Trains 1 and 3 above were combined, omitting Marblehead (tracks removed) and Topsfield. A new daily freight was assigned to Topsfield and return. Portsmouth service, trains 5 and 6, was now handled by one train on a two-day schedule, assuming the work of train 4. Train 2 continued. In sum: seven one-way trips replaced the former ten.

Lacking car counts, we cannot know the size of the trains between these two comparison dates, eight years apart; probably they got smaller. The author remembers a general perception among B&M employees that business was slowly but surely falling off, and that the McGinnis administration was to blame. In retrospect, it appears that the loss of business was reflective of a larger picture, especially poignant in New England, of the American economy moving away from its manufacturing roots at the same time that trucks were acquiring a larger share of the available business.

The Eastern Route has a varied palette of vistas along its 57 miles. The Boston area industrial trackage fascinates with its myriad freight houses and sidings; Swampscott brings an abrupt, head-long dive into thick foliage; and north of Beverly we have the generous, hilly sweep of North Shore farms and eventually, after Newburyport, we look across the salt marshes to the sparkling white sand of New Hampshire beaches. Of course, the mood of the trip changed with the season and the day's weather, but it was often a stunning ride.

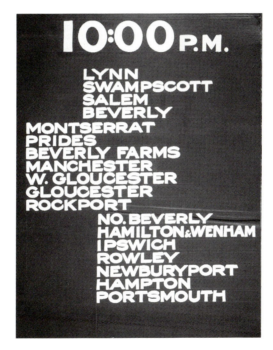

10:00 P.M.

LYNN
SWAMPSCOTT
SALEM
BEVERLY
MONTSERRAT
PRIDES
BEVERLY FARMS
MANCHESTER
W. GLOUCESTER
GLOUCESTER
ROCKPORT
NO. BEVERLY
HAMILTON & WENHAM
IPSWICH
ROWLEY
NEWBURYPORT
HAMPTON
PORTSMOUTH

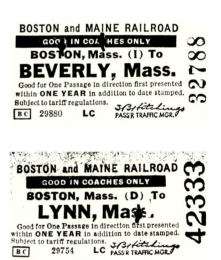

BOSTON and MAINE RAILROAD
GOOD IN COACHES ONLY
BOSTON, Mass. (I) To
BEVERLY, Mass.
Good for One Passage in direction first presented
within ONE YEAR in addition to date stamped.
Subject to tariff regulations.
BC   29880   LC   PASS'R TRAFFIC MGR.
32788

BOSTON and MAINE RAILROAD
GOOD IN COACHES ONLY
BOSTON, Mass. (D) To
LYNN, Mass.
Good for One Passage in direction first presented
within ONE YEAR in addition to date stamped.
Subject to tariff regulations.
BC   29754   LC   PASS'R TRAFFIC MGR.
42333

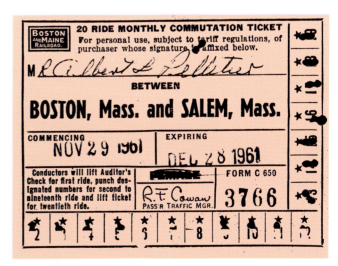

BOSTON AND MAINE RAILROAD.
20 RIDE MONTHLY COMMUTATION TICKET
For personal use, subject to tariff regulations, of
purchaser whose signature is affixed below.
MR Gilbert L Pelletier
BETWEEN
BOSTON, Mass. and SALEM, Mass.
COMMENCING   EXPIRING
NOV 29 1961   DEC 28 1961
Conductors will lift Auditor's
Check for first ride, punch des-   FORM C 650
ignated numbers for second to
nineteenth ride and lift ticket   R.F. Cowan   3766
for twentieth ride.   PASS'R TRAFFIC MGR.

Above left: Pickman Park in Salem was a remote location sought out by
only a few discerning photographers. RS-3 1535 passes the pond with an
afternoon freight for Boston in July 1964. **Top**: By August 1964 the
Talgo had lost one of its five three-car units to fire. Here it heads over
Beverly Drawbridge back to Boston for a second afternoon commuter run.
Note the unwashed band of dirt along the bottom edge of the train. Two
photos, Russell F. Munroe. **Above**: The roll sign for the 10:00 p.m. to
Rockport and Portsmouth shows how a few trains serviced both lines
simultaneously.

Left: On a gloomy March 6, 1969 a crew attempts to re-rail the front axle of the diesel locomotive's lead truck after it encountered ice at a crossing in Gloucester. Dana A. Story photo/Richard W. Symmes collection.

Below: A single northbound RDC arrives at Beverly in the bleakness of January 1964. Russell F. Munroe photo.

Right: In the distance is a yellow indication on the home signal, and Budd RDC 6117 will soon depart this spot, the sight of the former Ipswich depot, for Boston.

Below right: Budd RDC 6301 waits at Newburyport for the next run to Boston.

Below far right: A freight passes into a snowstorm at the end of double track in Wenham in January 1968. Three photos in deep winter by the intrepid Richard W. Symmes.

By the Sea

THE SAUGUS BRANCH

This ten-mile branch of the B&M began life in 1853, five years having passed since its charter date in 1848 by an independant company. Progress was slowed by a paucity of funding. Originally built to connect with the Boston & Maine at Malden, the line was changed slightly when the Eastern Railroad bought it and connected it to its own mainline at Everett. The Eastern had feared losing its Lynn freight business to the B&M. At the time of the acquisition, a short connection was built from the original terminus at Lynn Common to the main-

line at Lynn, resulting in two, nearly parallel, lines between Lynn and Everett. Since there was no other public transportation then, these rails were an important and vital source of transportation for a rapidly growing population. Heavy patronage mandated the double tracking of the branch in 1891-92.

The high ridership is born out by the presence of *fifteen* stations in its short length, and a train's repeated stopping and starting is reflected in 1950s timetables. A Boston-Lynn trip via the Saugus Branch consumed

Stanley W. Cook has captured the rural essence of the Saugus Branch while it was still under steam in the early fifties. **Above**: *a lady in red awaits the 7:22 a.m. train for Boston at West Street on April 17, 1953. Mogul 1427 is on the point.* **Below**: *A five-car train arrives at Franklin Park May 8, 1952. Note the gravestone-like crossing gate control device at left.* **Right**: *In a classic scene, a Lynn-bound commuter train of wooden coaches pulls over the grade crossing at Cliftondale on May 23, 1952.*

some 51 minutes, versus 20 via the mainline with no stops. Surprisingly, all 15 stations were still being served when passenger service was ended in May 1958.

From the peak of activity in the earlier years of the century, when there were some 19 trains over the branch into Boston, service had declined markedly by the time of our period of interest. The Saturday round trip ended in 1948, leaving three morning inbounds and two evening outbounds on the weekdays. One of the three morning trains was gone by September 1950, leaving the two round trips which lasted until the end of service.

Freight service was handled by a daily local which left Boston about 10 a.m., taking most of the day to work the branch and then the General Electric River Works before returning to Boston. The line was single tracked after passenger service ended, and in the following years the weeds grew up thickly as freight business gradually dropped away. A major resurgence of freight business—gravel, specifically—took place in the late sixties when a short spur was built from just East of Linden out onto the Lynn Marsh, for the purpose of building a new section of Interstate Route 95. Four trains daily, 60 cars each, brought massive quantities of gravel to the site. A change of Governors brought revised thinking about such environmentally questionable road projects, and the endeavor was halted, only partially complete, three and a half million cubic yards of gravel having been brought from Bow, New Hampshire.

Then once again the Saugus Branch fell into a state of quiet repose.

By the Sea
TWO BRANCHES TO MARBLEHEAD

A debutant party was given by Mr. and Mrs. Harold D. Hodgkinson of Boston and Marblehead for their daughter Charlotte. The party was given aboard a special train which left the North Station on December 20, 1950 at 9:30 p.m. The train consisted of engine 3235 (4-4-2), combine 2139, baggage car, six 500 series coaches and caboose 4336 and was routed to Marblehead. The baggage car served as a diner and the caboose as the reception room. The entire party had old time train travel as the motif, complete with the confidence man, politician, and the candy butcher. The 500 guests aboard were treated to a grand time, and at Marblehead were greeted by a brass band which escorted the party to the Town Hall for an old fashioned country dance.

Callboy
Massachusetts Bay Railroad Enthusiasts

After the Eastern Railroad reached Salem in August 1838, Marblehead citizens eyed the new service jealously. As always, they were people of action (the U. S. Navy was begun here and it was Marblehead men who rowed Washington across the Delaware), and they bought $40,000 in shares from the Eastern to cover the construction costs. Service on the Marblehead Branch began December 10, 1839 with a 12½ cent fare for the three and a half mile ride to Salem, ending forever the local stagecoach service. Eventually the intrusion of the trolley would, in turn, cut into rail business dramatically. By 1922 there were just three daily round trips, only one in 1933. By the end of World War II there was one evening train to Salem (curiously there was no inbound counterpart) and the last of these left one night in 1954 (This was actually a deadhead move of Boston-Marblehead commuter equipment, bound for the North Street Yard in Salem to spend the night).

Direct service to Boston did not come so easily. Town efforts in 1847 and 1865 to have another branch built came to nothing. But in 1871, as a town meeting vote on action was imminent, the Eastern Railroad stepped in and announced it would build the line. Its motives were not altruistic: it needed the passenger revenues desperately (there never would be any freight service on the line because it was completely residential). The rival Boston & Maine was literally giving them a run for their money, encroaching on their turf at Salem, Newburyport, Portsmouth, and on into Maine. As we have seen, the Eastern gave up in 1884 when leased by the B&M.

The Swampscott Branch—as this new four and a half mile piece of single track was called—was completed in October 1873 with three other stations along the way: Phillips Beach, Beach Bluff, and Clifton. A fourth station — Devereux — was added a year later, and all four were paid for by subscriptions from adjoining landowners.

Marblehead had lots of depots. The first one, a simple affair, was not deemed grand enough for the Swampscott Branch when that was completed. The resulting second, more elaborate depot burned to the ground in 1877, as did the third depot in 1886. Taking no chances, the B&M built the fourth depot of brick, and it lasted a healthy 72 years.

Marblehead, with its splendid old architecture and revolutionary war heritage, its almost total lack of industry save for that associated with yachting, and Marblehead Neck—the home of yacht clubs and the unconspicuously wealthy—has long been a popular residence for the Boston executive. Thus, traditionally it could support a considerable volume of commuter train service: 12 round trips in 1933, ten in 1947, six in 1951 (the Mystic Bridge had opened, easing the auto drive into town), five and a half in 1953, six and a half in 1955, three and a half in 1958. It was bad enough that service had by this time been cut to the bone (ridership was indeed down badly), but the B&M further compounded the inconvenience by requiring a change at Lynn for the final train departing Boston at 6:15 p.m. Of all the indignities. Lynn, indeed!

Marblehead has the distinction of hosting the B&M's final revenue steam runs. On July 23, 1956, Pacifics 3662 and 3654 each led morning commuter trains to Boston. During 1955 and 1956 it was possible to see three forms of motive power in Marblehead: steam, diesel, and RDC. Three years later all service ended on an overcast Friday, June 13, 1959, as Budd RDCs 6127, 6146, and 6210 let out a long, deafening series of short whistle blasts on their last ever trip out of Marblehead.

Above: *The front half of this vintage steam train has crossed the Forest River Bridge into Salem from Marblehead, deadheading commuter coaches to Salem for the night. Neighborhood children are swimming on this beautiful June 3, 1952 afternoon, the brakeman is about to step down to flag the Lafayette Street crossing, and all's right with the world. Russell F. Munroe photo.*

Below: *When Mr. Munroe learned that steam would end in Marblehead, he made frequent trips to the town during the winter, spring, and summer of 1956 to document the final days. His brilliant work is a fine record of this bygone era. Here, a morning train takes empty cars past the Tower School to begin a commuter run.*

Left above: Three Budds depart Phillips Beach for Marblehead on Thursday, June 12, 1959, the penultimate day of passenger service. This station was never updated in the new post-war ocher and maroon colors, keeping its light gray and dark green to the end.

Left below: Quite a rig, this weed-spraying train! Steam powered, eight cars in all, a caboose on the head end, and special tank cars with the Minute Man herald in white, the equipment is headed past Gilbert & Cole Lumber toward Marblehead Depot on the Salem track.

Right: The commuter business is still robust as B&M Pacific 3624 brings a six-car train around the wye toward Marblehead in the summer of 1956.

Below: Two 4-6-2 Pacifics face off early one winter morning in 1956. Four photos, Russell F. Munroe.

THE GLOUCESTER BRANCH

In the potentially hazardous game of racing railroad trains, only Mr. and Mrs. John Lowell Gardner, Jr., had both the means and the merriment to apply the maxim about joining 'em if you can't beat 'em. The Gardners of Boston were old summerers of Beverly, and one day at the height of the 1891 season, being sports, they reserved seats on the maiden run of a new tallyho from Pride's Crossing to the Myopia Hunt Club in Hamilton. They missed the train at Boston, however. An hour later, as the gala coach-and-four was about to pull out, down the track thundered a locomotive of the B&M, belching smoke and steam, while screaming, bell in urgent clanging. This apparition screeched to a grinding stop at the Pride's station, and out of the cab jumped Jack to help his Isabella down from her seat beside the fireman. All in the nick of time. Arriving at North Station and a missed train, the Gardners had hired a spare engine on the spot, which was something you could do in those days if you had the right connections to rectify the wrong ones.

Joseph E. Garland
Boston's Gold Coast

The Eastern Railroad, having made a great success of its line between East Boston and Portsmouth, perceived a potential for a healthy profit in the shore communities beyond Beverly; the first section opened to Manchester on August 3, 1847, and the second to Gloucester four months later on December 1. When Rockport residents failed to persuade the Eastern to extend the line 3.7 miles to their town, two subsequent private ventures were chartered before sufficient capital could be raised and construction could begin. Service finally began November 4, 1861. The Eastern bought the line in 1868 after seven years of contract operation.

The Gloucester Branch opened as a single track line, the change-over to double track occupying the 17 year period from 1894 to 1911. Although double track was completed to a point just east of Gloucester Depot, this was cut back during the late 1950s to a point designated as "Wilson," one third mile west of Gloucester Depot. While Salem Tower controlled Beverly Junction once electric operation replaced the Armstrong machines, the Branch itself was controlled by automatic block signals.

In the early years, Rockport trains were joined at Beverly to mainline trains. Although this practice stopped after 1864, when Rockport trains ran through to Boston, it reappeared again in the 1950s when RDCs

proliferated on the Branch. In 1958 there were seven such split trains operating. The B&M had reached an agreement with the unions (Engineers and Firemen) which permitted the railroad to operate single-unit RDC trains with one man in the cab. A two-car RDC train originating in Boston, with both an engineer and fireman in the cab, would be split enroute at Beverly, one car going to Gloucester, the other to Newburyport or Portsmouth, each piloted by a lone engineer. The B&M tinkered constantly with the practice; the point of separation and connection became Salem Station in 1960, except for the late evening trains, for which Northey Point (just east of Salem Tower) was used.

Once ridership required the use of more than two RDCs, the whole operation lost its usefulness, and trains for each of the two separate destinations were run through from Boston. The single such train remaining from 1961 was the midnight train, two RDCs as far as Salem, single cars to Rockport and Portsmouth.

Stations at Manchester and Gloucester were the original two stops on the branch, with Beverly Farms (originally West Farms) added about 1857. Rockport opened in 1861, Montserrat and Prides Crossing following in the 1880s. Later came West Manchester, Magnolia ("where for years carriages from the now-forgotten Oceanside Hotel met the trains," according to writer Ed Brown) and West Gloucester. Although the last service to Magnolia ended in 1949—a single, summer only stop in the morning, 7:07 a.m. inbound, 9:48 a.m. outbound—timetables listed the station through 1952.

Like so much of New England, the Gloucester Branch is enveloped in a sprawling web of lush green foliage in the warm months. When once Boston's North Shore was known as the "Gold Coast," a time when many of the city's wealthy power brokers found it desirable to build large estates there, hidden in the crannies of the resplendent countryside, the Boston & Maine instituted the *Flying Fisherman* for their exclusive use. Running non-stop between Boston and Beverly Farms from 1892 to 1920 with a parlor car consist, the train was available to those chosen individuals who could afford the $100 season pass, a charge levied over and above the parlor car fees. Those just content to watch it pass, waiting for their own train of mere coaches, referred to it as the "Dude Train." Joseph E. Garland speaks amusingly of the train in *Boston's Gold Coast*:

Times changed, and the Dude Train, having survived the Great War, died with the peace, to the dismay of one devotee, whose chauffeur for years had been dropping him off at the Magnolia depot

B&M train 2558 behind Pacific 3672 steams over Manchester Drawbridge on March 26, 1950 with a Boston train of four assorted coaches. Donald G. Hills photo.

in the morning, then driving hell-bent over the road to Boston and picking him up at North Station and on to the office—as Robert Rapp tells it—so that he shouldn't miss his game of cards en route. Presumably this mad race was reversed in the afternoon.

In later years the B&M ran a similar, late afternoon train to the Gloucester Branch, running express from Boston to Montserrat and making local stops for the remainder of the trip to Rockport. Its evening departure from Boston was just before 5 p.m., its morning arrival a few minutes before 9 a.m. (9 a.m. on the dot beginning in 1955). It was one of a very few trains to stop at West Manchester, a station which saw its last service at the close of the 1955 summer season.

A touch of class was added in 1951 when the Railroad started calling the train *The Cape Ann*, but there was no special upgrading of equipment. By 1955, Salem (as a flag stop) and Beverly had been added to the *Cape Ann*, and because Budd RDCs were now covering the schedule, the time over the road—one hour, two minutes—was actually an improvement by two minutes from earlier schedules. Following the summer of 1958 the *Cape Ann* name was dropped altogether, as was the "express" schedule.

The Gloucester Branch freight tonnage was modest in postwar years, yet still profitable. *The Camel*, its name the product of forgotten B&M lore, plied the line six days a week from the war years through at least 1954, but by 1962 this was reduced to three days a week[7]. Most of the business was at Gloucester, with a few cars to Rockport and Manchester.

Some have lamented that, for a railroad so tantalizingly close to wonderful seaside vistas, the Gloucester Branch affords the curious rider pitifully few of them. Once on the Branch itself, past Beverly Junction, one first gets a glimpse of the Atlantic just east of Beverly Farms. The small inlet traversed by Manchester Drawbridge provides another brief look. Approaching Gloucester on a long, high fill, the road crosses the Annisquam River at Gloucester Drawbridge, the location rife with tangy, salt air. Once into Gloucester proper, though, the line becomes single track and winds through bucolic woodland settings to Rockport where a brief walk brings one to the charms of the art colony and the sea itself.

Of course, this generally inland passage has spared the line all manner of storm damage through the years. One has only to examine the checkered history of the New Haven's Shore Line to see how vulnerable a true shore-hugging railroad can be.

Ed Brown grew up in Beverly Farms, and his recollections are the kind touching a nerve in so many of us who remember steam railroading in New England:

Among my early memories of the years just after World War II was meeting the steam engines which brought my father home to Beverly Farms from his job in Boston. (Oh, to have been more knowledgeable and camera-equipped in those days!) From my quiet backyard a half-mile from the tracks I could hear those tough and dependable Pacifics blast off for Boston, slip occasionally on the grade at Prides when the rails were wet, the whistle for Paradise Crossing in the distant woods before fading out of hearing[8].

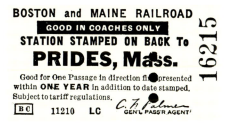

Above left: *A lovely autumn scene in a rock cut on the way to Rockport.
We hope that is a B&M employee astraddle the gondola's far corner on
Work Extra 864. H. Bentley Crouch photo.*

Above: *It is oh so very early and mighty cold on December 15, 1963 as a
lone Budd traverses the fill dividing Gloucester Harbor from the
Annisquam River.*

Left: *A maroon GP-7 and a blue caboose are headed for Rockport to pick
up cars in March 1962. Two photos, Russell F. Munroe.*

Right: *Semaphores still functioned between Gloucester and Rockport into
the early sixties. RWJ photo.*

Above: B&M Train 11, the Kennebec, speeds past milepost 98 approaching Wilmington Junction on its non-stop, two-hour dash to Portland from where it will continue to Bangor via Augusta over the Maine Central. The two roads pooled their mainline equipment, often mixing stainless steel coaches with older cars. The fourth car is probably a parlor car. Donald G. Hills photo. *Below*: The occasion of this festive gathering at Dover, New Hampshire is the last official steam run on the B&M, on April 22, 1956. Pacific 3713—still in existence today—did the honors. Dwight A. Smith photo.

IV

HEADING DOWN EAST

The Western Route of the Portland Division

...the Portland run is like an old-fashioned washboard rather than a billiard table. The line is one wrinkle, upgrade and downgrade, after another. It's a shore line, yes, but it's crammed with grades approaching 1 percent... ridges of rock, sweeping down from the White Mountains, haven't flattened out even as they approach their junction with the ocean. The Portland Division is the pet... It has the railroad's best equipment and it's the division the big brass cares most about.

R. M. Neal
High Green and the Barkpeelers

The Boston & Maine Railroad was created June 27, 1835 as a New Hampshire corporation, its purpose to continue building trackage already constructed north of Wilmington, Massachusetts (where it met the Boston & Lowell) by the Boston & Portland and its two predecessors. The B&P and B&M merged in 1842, the year tracks reached the Maine state line. A year later the B&M had established operations between Boston and Portland through agreements with roads at either end, signalling the beginning of its serious rivalry with the Eastern Railroad which had begun running its trains to Portland in 1842.

Both the B&M and the Eastern utilized the Portland, Saco & Portsmouth Railroad for access to Portland, and though the arrangement—sensible as it was—was fraught with problems, it continued for 30 years. After the Eastern and the Maine Central attempted to corner exclusive use of this connection (the Eastern refusing to wait for late B&M trains at South Berwick),

the B&M completed its own line to Portland in 1873.

On the south end at Wilmington, the B&M soon found that it was too important a system to rely on the Boston & Lowell for entry to Boston, and thus built its own line through to Haymarket Square, Boston in 1845. Also, nine and a half miles of track between Ballardvale and Andover were relocated in 1846 to provide better service to Lawrence.

With the leasing of the Eastern by the B&M in 1884 and the eventual merger in 1890, the redundancies in trackage caused by the unbridled competition began a sorting out process which would occupy the next 50 years. Thus the Eastern's line to Portland would eventually be supplanted by that of the B&M, the last through train to Portland via Portsmouth ceasing in 1951.

For passenger revenue, the Portland Division was far and away the B&M's biggest success from very early on, especially in the summer when hordes of tourists visited beaches and other Maine attractions. The streamline age on the B&M began in April 1935 with the arrival of Unit 6000, immediately named the *Flying Yankee*, for express service between Boston, Portland and Bangor. Its only problem was that it was such a success that it couldn't begin to handle the demand with its fixed consist, though it stayed on the same run until May 1944.

The Boston & Maine and the Maine Central each bought shiny fleets of streamlined cars right after World War II, along with a stable of E-7s in maroon and gold to head this important varnish. Each road purchased eight coaches, two combines, and two diners to service the Boston to Bangor business. Later in 1954 the

B&M added four stainless sleepers as well. The Bangor & Aroostook took delivery of three such coaches in 1949—one of these often running through to Boston—and two sleepers for *Gull* service in early 1955.

The Boston-Bangor daytime varnish carried the names *Flying Yankee, Pine Tree,* and *Kennebec.* The *Gull* operated through sleeping cars to a variety of northern destinations, including Bangor and Calais (MEC), Van Buren (BAR), Saint John, NB (MEC, CP) and Halifax, NS (MEC, CP, CN). The *State of Maine* carried several sleepers each night between New York City and Portland via Worcester, meeting the Portland mainline at Lowell Junction. Popular summer trains included the daytime *East Wind* (New York to Portland), the *Down Easter* (sleeping cars from New York to Rockland and Waterville, Maine and Plymouth, New Hampshire), and the famous *Bar Harbor* (sleeping cars from Washington to Ellsworth, and from both Philadelphia and New York to Bangor, Ellsworth, Portland and Rockland).

In spite of the tremendous pride the B&M took in these trains, patronage began to slide precipitously in the fifties. The McGinnis administration sold the stainless steel equipment to the Wabash, with the Budd RDCs covering what was left of the daytime through trains (the four stainless sleepers remained under B&M ownership—though sometimes used elsewhere—until 1966 when they were sold to Canadian National). The *Gull* appears (though it is not clear from the timetable) to have lost its sleeping cars in 1959, though a train on that schedule continued through 1960. The April 24, 1960 timetable very cleverly obfuscates the fact that there is indeed a southbound train to Boston from the Maritimes. It's easy to blame the railroad for discouraging business, yet in large measure the customers were going by other means of travel.

Nineteen sixty four was the final year for passenger service to Portland from Boston, with a single weekday round trip and three round trips on Saturdays and Sundays. Service north of Portland had long since become a memory.

Freight, on the other hand, continued to thrive on

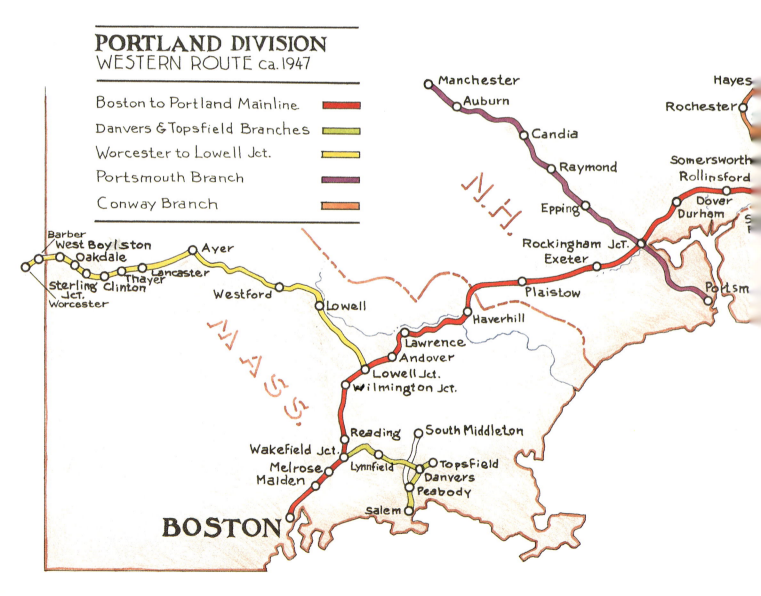

PORTLAND DIVISION
WESTERN ROUTE ca. 1947

Boston to Portland Mainline
Danvers & Topsfield Branches
Worcester to Lowell Jct.
Portsmouth Branch
Conway Branch

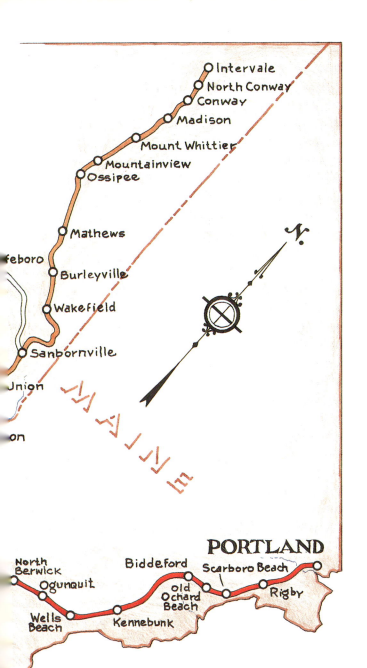

the Portland mainline, as the 1954 table shows at the bottom of the page. Yet, eight years later in 1962, activity was somewhat less. Of the two freights operating between Boston and Portland, only one pair continued. Rigby-Mechanicville trains were the same, but the Rigby-Worcester pair, N1 and P2, has disappeared from the schedule. The reduction is significant, representing one third of the 1954 trains.

The picture is different for the Portland Division local freights:

1954 Scheduled Local Freights

From	To	Departure
Lawrence	Merrimac-Dover and return	9:10 a.m.
Lawrence	Lowell Jct-Manchester & return	7:30 a.m.
Manchester	Portsmouth-Fremont & return	8:15 a.m.
Rigby	Dover and return	8:40 a.m.
Dover	Wolfboro-Intervale-N. Conway	6:30 a.m.
N. Conway	Intervale-Dover	7:30 a.m.

Compare this with the 1962 schedule, and its reworked activity:

1962 Schedule Local Freights

From	To	Departure
Lawrence	Grenier A.F.B. and return	9:00 a.m.
Lawrence	South Middleton and return	9:00 a.m.
Dover	Wolfboro-Intervale-N. Conway	7:00 a.m.
N. Conway	Dover	7:00 a.m.
Dover	Rochester-Rigby and return	8:30 a.m.
Dover	Lowell Junction and return	10:00 p.m.

1954 Scheduled Mainline Freights

No.	From	To		Departs	Name
B11	Boston	Bangor		7:20 p.m.	
B12	Bangor	Boston	Leave Rigby	11:00 p.m.	
BP5	Boston	Rigby		10:00 p.m.	
PB4	Rigby	Boston		6:30 p.m.	
M6	New York	Portland	Leave Worcester	4:00 a.m.	*Maine Bullet*
M7	Portland	New York		3:45 p.m.	*Maine Bullet*
PM1	Rigby	Mechanicville		12:30 a.m.	*The Clipper*
MP2	Mechanicville	Portland		10:00 a.m.	*Forest City*
PM3	Rigby	Mechanicville		7:00 a.m.	
MP4	Mechanicville	Portland		4:00 p.m.	
N1	Rigby	Worcester		3:30 a.m.	*The Newsboy*
P2	Worcester	Rigby		10:30 a.m.	*Dirigo*

The McGinnis administration implemented a major operational change in June 1959 when it routed all Portland Division West trains over the New Hampshire Division from Boston to Wilmington, and over the three-mile, single track *Wildcat* from Wilmington to Wilmington Junction (the original B&M route when it made its entry to Boston via the Boston & Lowell). B&M trains then used this new route until 1979. The plan was much derided by employees and railfans at the time it was begun, yet it seems to have made economic sense all the same.

The Portland Division West, the great "high iron" on the Boston & Maine, would continue to hold its own through the difficult sixties and seventies. It is, after all, the only route from the south into northern New England.

In another generation, who knows? Perhaps it will sing to the hum of mainline passenger varnish once again.

Above: *After this steam excursion stopped at Rockingham Junction to take on water on June 8, 1952 the water plug could not be turned off. Later, when the return trip was ready to depart south from Portland, a freight derailment caused the excursion to be rerouted—sans steam—down the* Eastern Route behind an E-7. Russell F. Munroe photo. **Below**: *Intervale to Boston train 2914 sweeps down the mainline approaching Salem Street in North Wilmington with several head- and rear-end revenue cars behind P2 Pacific 3639 in July 1950. Donald G. Hills photo.*

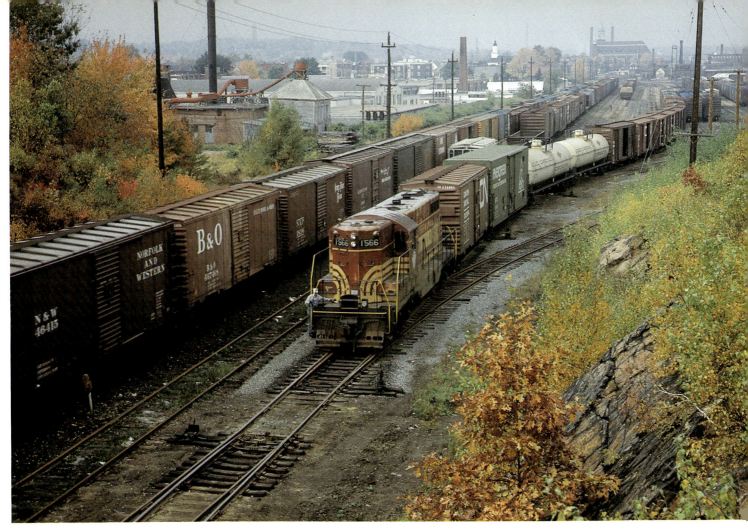

Above: Amidst resplendent fall color, train D6, the Dover-Lawrence local, works the South Lawrence Yard behind GP-7 1566, regularly assigned this run for several years. H. Bentley Crouch photo.

Below: Russell F. Munroe was standing on the Route 1 overpass at Biddeford on July 3, 1964 when he photographed this southbound freight behind Bluebird 1726 with an old maroon B unit.

6:20 P.M.
ANDOVER
LAWRENCE
HAVERHILL
EXETER
DOVER
NORTH BERWICK
WELLS BEACH
KENNEBUNK
BIDDEFORD
OLD ORCHARD
PORTLAND
BRUNSWICK
AUGUSTA
WATERVILLE, ME.
BANGOR
VANCEBORO (AROOSTOOK COUNTY)
ST. JOHN, N.B.
MONCTON
HALIFAX

The 6:20 p.m. roll sign shows signs of a fast-deteriorating Gull.

Left: Behind Maine Central E-7 711, B&M train 134 from Portland to Boston is at milepost 98 with two stainless coaches, an "American Flyer" coach, and a smoker-combine. Only the nose herald distinguishes the 711's paint scheme from that of its B&M brothers, and it is impossible to tell whether the stainless coaches are B&M or MEC without seeing the letterboard. Donald G. Hills photo.

Below: Pacific 3713 sweeps majestically around the curve at Newmarket, New Hampshire. Though it looks like a typical New England winter day, it is actually April 22, 1956, and this is the last official steam run. Norton D. Clark photo.

Right: Many unusual stations grace the New England landscape, and this one at East Kingston, New Hampshire looks just like a colonial home. Wayne D. Allen photo/J. Emmons Lancaster collection.

Center: B&M 44-tonner 117 is switching at Biddeford, July 3, 1961. Russell F. Munroe photo.

Bottom: Portland Union Station was a magnificent granite edifice; it was a great loss indeed when it was demolished in 1961. Here it is during its heyday of the mid forties. Art Forrestal photo/collection of Sullivan photo.

Above: We've got the highball from the Rigby car knocker this beautiful April 15, 1977, and our three sharp-looking GP-38s are ready to take our freight to Mechanicville. Herman Shaner photo/J. Emmons Lancaster collection. **Below**: Street running is sometimes neglected by rail photographers because it isn't glamorous. Russell F. Munroe found B&M switcher 1223 working Portland Terminal trackage on Commercial Street, October 10, 1983. **Above right**: At Portland Union Station head-end cars from the State of Maine are being serviced. That baggage and express car from the Florida East Coast is a long way from home this July 3, 1961. Russell F. Munroe photo.

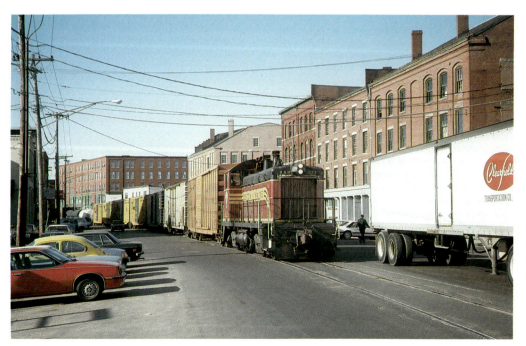

Right: The Gull traversed four railroads on its daily trek between Boston and Halifax—Boston & Maine, Maine Central, Canadian Pacific, and Canadian National (five if you include Bangor & Aroostook connections to northern Maine)—and the train regularly carried equipment from all these. Here it is southbound at Congress Street, Portland, about to enter Union Station behind Maine Central E-7s 709 and 705, the latter in the newer, pine green paint scheme. Of interest are the crossing tender's tower at the left and the ball signal in the center. Donald G. Hills photo.

DANVERS AND TOPSFIELD

The maze of rail lines in the Danvers area was certainly among the most complex and dense on the B&M system, perhaps the premiere example of the vicious competition among railroad enterpreneurs in the last half of the nineteenth century. One has only to glance at the map, opposite, to note the ridiculous density of the trackage. Even as relatively small a community as Danvers was still served by two separate commuter rail branches as late as 1958 (and there were nine stations within the town limits).

A few explanatory facts should help to clarify the picture. The Lawrence Branch was owned by the Eastern Railroad, as was the South Reading Branch. The Salem Branch was owned by the Boston & Lowell Railroad, while the Newburyport Branch was that of the Boston & Maine. By 1887 all trackage was controlled by the Boston & Maine, and from that date a gradual pruning began, reflecting the true economic possibilities of the trackage.

In 1926 most of the South Reading Branch was abandoned, affecting only freight operation, while on the Lawrence Branch all passenger service was cut back to Danvers.

In 1939 the freight-only Salem Branch lost its trackage from South Middleton to Wilmington Junction. On the Newburyport Branch, passenger service north of Topsfield ended after 1942 and the track was abandoned. By 1949, the level of passenger service was still respectable in the Danvers area: on the Newburyport Branch there was one train each to Boston from Topsfield and Danvers, and three from Wakefield Center. The Lawrence Branch provided Danvers to Boston service via Salem with four inbound trains, two in the morning and two in the evening.

Nine years later in May, 1958, the McGinnis administration eliminated the last two trains remaining on the Boston-Salem-Danvers route. Then, in June, 1959, the last two Danvers via Wakefield Junction trains were cancelled, ending 112 years of operation. [Note: the branch from Salem to Danvers was actually part of the Portland Division East. It is included here and on the Chapter IV map to conserve space.]

Stanley W. Cook captured the action in these three photos. **Above**: *Danvers, having been a busy junction in earlier years, was a maze of order boards and manual interlocking signals. Train 2413 has arrived from Boston via Salem at 5:05 p.m. on August 18, 1953.* **Right**: *The Wakefield Junction station agent can be seen in the bay window, warning the photographer that the time is 5:49 p.m., and southbound train 170 is due on the near track at 5:50 for Boston. In the background, the Danvers train has just taken the branch behind Pacific 3659.* **Above right**: *Seconds later Cook crossed to the main platform to photograph the speeding southbound train.*

Railroad trackage around Danvers prior to 1887. John Signor map.

Above: GP-7 1556 is switching a tank car on the Hebb Leather track in Danversport. Russell F. Munroe photo.

Left: Four-car B&M RDC train with 6137 trailing heads through the manual interlocking at West Peabody toward Danvers from Wakefield Junction in July 1959. Russell F. Munroe photo.

Above right: Its day's work of switching done, RS-3 1535 crosses the quiet expanse of the Ipswich River in Topsfield on its way back to the mainline at Salem. Richard W. Symmes photo.

Below right: In a stunning winter portrait, switcher 800 plows the South Middleton Branch in March 1963. Russell F. Munroe photo.

The famed East Wind *at Barber, Massachusetts on a bright 1941 day. This superb shot is rare indeed. Not only does it show the vivid yellow and silver scheme which lasted only three years, but it reveals a consist of at least ten cars. On the point is B&M Mountain 4113, the Black Arrow; only the 4100s could make it from Worcester to Portland without stopping for water. During 1940-42, the train traversed* Pennsylvania, New Haven, and Boston & Maine *trackage, with a coach and diner sent through to Bangor over the Maine Central on the* Pine Tree Limited. *After the war the train was revived intermittently through 1955, but never with these colors or as much dedicated service. Stanley Smith photo/Norton D. Clark collection.*

This special section of B&M trackage is comprised of three separate, shorter lines used in tandem to provide an efficient link for heavy east-west tonnage running on the Fitchburg and Portland Divisions.

The first of these to open was the 9-mile Lowell & Lawrence Railroad, chartered in 1846 to provide Lowell citizens—who already had service to Boston via the Boston & Lowell—a new routing via the Boston & Maine at Lawrence. In 1858 the Boston & Lowell took control.

The second of the three lines was the Stony Brook Railroad. Lowell had been enjoying rail service since 1835, and with the passage of time its denizens cast a jealous eye on newer services between Boston and Fitchburg in 1845 and between Worcester and Nashua in 1848, wondering how they might have more expeditious connections to the south and west. These desires led to the opening of a new 13-mile line from North Chelmsford on the B&L through the Stony Brook Valley to Ayer Junction on the Fitchburg Railroad in July 1848. This new enterprise, the Stony Brook Railroad, was then immediately leased to the Nashua & Lowell.

The third of the lines was the Worcester & Nashua, which also opened in 1848. It began at Worcester, utilizing a less-than-a-mile branch built in 1844 north to Lincoln Square from the Boston & Worcester, and went north 28 miles to Ayer.

These three independent sections did not form an important entity until 1911, because in November 1874 trackage was opened between Nashua and Rochester, New Hampshire, completing a direct rail link between Worcester and Portland via another route. Though it became the Worcester, Nashua & Portland Division of the B&M in 1886, ownership by the powerful B&M did not alleviate its considerable problems: single track, no signals, rugged terrain and very steep grades, all of these resulting in frequent and expensive accidents.

So in 1911 the B&M began downgrading the WN&P Division, routing some of its through freights via the Stony Brook and Lowell Branches. This was such a success that more and more trains were so routed until 1924 when through freights via the WN&P were discontinued.

Worcester to Lowell Junction was double-tracked in 1929 and in that year became the first CTC installation in New England. June 1946 saw 30 daily trains pass over the Stony Brook portion of the line: two local and six express passenger (the year-round *State of Maine*, and the summertime *Bar Harbor* and *East Wind*) and two local and 20 mainline freights. One special highlight was the annual summer passage of camp trains from Philadelphia and New York to Maine.

The last local passenger service on the Stony Brook ended in April 1953, a single round trip between Worcester and Lowell (Timetables in the post WWII era list no stations whatever on the Lowell Branch). Curiously, the B&M advertised train No. 521, Boston-Worcester via Ayer, in the timetables from 1953 through 1956, as making at stop at Clinton at 11:19 p.m. The train carried Railway Express cars—Federal Reserve cash to Chicago being one significant commodity—and perhaps the Clinton stop was a late-night accommodation for theater goers, since Clinton had no night service past the rush hour. There was no comparable eastbound service in the passenger timetable.

The double track proved less and less necessary, and

so the second track was removed in 1957. The famous and long-enduring *State of Maine* lasted through October 1960, its passing leaving only the *Montrealer-Washingtonian* in the B&M's once-lusty roster of name trains.

Nonetheless, this 53-mile triple branch continued to provide the backbone for east-west freight on the B&M as traffic more frequently circumvented Boston. It still operates successfully and profitably in this fashion today.

Two shots of Worcester Station by Stephen R. Payne. **Below***: Mogul 1468 simmers on the Peterboro local while express is loaded.* **Bottom***: Some fine detail of the depot at street level. Do you suppose the Villanova was a favorite place for the crews? Mogul 1427 has another Peterboro train.*

Left: David C. Bartlett found this B&M 0-6-0 at Sterling.

Below: Color shots of B&M Mountains are rare. Stephen R. Payne made this excellent freight shot at Sterling on February 16, 1951.

Above right: PM-3, a Portland-Mechanicville freight, pulls around the East Wye at Lowell Junction in 1950 behind FT 4218 A&B and F-2A 4260. Donald G. Hills photo.

Below right: Dana D. Goodwin was on hand to witness a famous annual event on July 3, 1949—the southbound return of an empty camp train, this one behind Pacific 3698. Courtesy of the Boston & Maine Railroad Historical Society.

THE PORTSMOUTH BRANCH

The 40 mile line from Portsmouth to Manchester, New Hampshire actually began its life in a different location. It was chartered as the Portsmouth & Concord in 1848, completed in 1852, and renamed Concord & Portsmouth in 1855. Its charter allowed for the construction of a branch to Manchester, as a means of competing with the Concord Railroad which up to then held a monopoly on all traffic. In order to complete construction, the C&P had to borrow $50,000 from the CRR (the Manchester & Lawrence was unable to help), so when it went bankrupt in 1859 the Concord RR leased it. A branch from Candia to Manchester was built and the trackage to Suncook removed, thus ending any possibility as competition to the Concord RR.

Right: *Portsmouth was another of the unique New England depots, still very much alive with Railway Express Agency business when this shot was taken in the early fifties. Ben Perry photo/Joseph Shaw collection.*

Below: *The combine on the tail end of the Portsmouth-Manchester mixed train carried a caboose number and caboose handrails. Joseph Snopek collection.*

Far right: *You can almost smell the wind in the pines. RS-3s 1510 and 1507 are just west of Raymond, New Hampshire on April 29, 1969 with train C10, the Concord-Portsmouth local freight. H. Bentley Crouch photo.*

During the 1940s and 1950s a local freight worked the Portsmouth Branch six days a week from Manchester. From 1961 it ran five days a week and in 1962 the point of origin became Concord.

The branch carried two passenger round trips (often covered by gas cars), between Portsmouth and Concord, mornings and evenings, six days a week for many years, providing connections to Boston-bound trains at three points: Manchester on the New Hampshire Mainline, Rockingham on the Portland Western, and Portsmouth on the Portland Eastern. The September 1952 timetable reflects a reduction to a single such train, mornings westbound, evenings eastbound. The train was cut back from Concord to Manchester after the summer of 1954, and by the following April the train was further downgraded to a mixed train, with over one half hour added to the schedule. This consisted of an aging combine (carrying a caboose number) on the hind end of the local freight.

Considering how drastically the McGinnis administration had cut into passenger service, it is a miracle that the train still appeared in the June 1958 timetable, which had gotten pretty thin by then. Still, it did carry revenue freight.

THE CONWAY BRANCH

For a companionable, chatty ride, go with the Bark Peelers. That means a trip on the North Conway Branch, up from Dover into the very midst of the White Mountains... their appeal doesn't come from their size, for they aren't impressively tall. The highest, Mount Washington, is only 6,283 feet... Yet their winter storms have demanded the life of more than one climber whose enthusiasm outstripped his judgement and experience.

R. M. Neal
High Green and the Bark Peelers

Rails to upper middle New Hampshire came about because transportation was needed for the state's timber and mineral resources, as well as to provide convenient and fast travel to the White Mountains' popular summer resorts.

The Mt. Washington Cog Railway reached the summit of Mt. Washington on July 3, 1869, the first railroad to be built in the immediate area. Its sole purpose was to carry tourists up the mountain. Smelling potential profits in carrying passengers there for this and the growing hotel business, in 1874 the Boston, Concord & Montreal built east from Littleton into the mountains to Bretton Woods-Fabyan. One year later the Portland & Ogdensburg reached Bretton Woods-Fabyan—on its way to the Great Lakes—with the completion of its line through Crawford Notch. In 1876 the BC&M extended its tracks to the Base Station at Mount Washington.

The third railroad to reach the White Mountains in the 1870s was the Portsmouth, Great Falls & Conway Railroad. Earlier, as the Great Falls and Conway, this road reached Union by 1854, where construction stopped because of financial difficulties. Operation of trains was even suspended for a time in 1858. The Eastern Railroad—with a serious financial interest—exercised its influence to get things moving again. 1865 saw the chartering of the Portsmouth, Great Falls & Conway; construction finally resumed in 1871, the year in which tracks reached Conway, and in 1872 the line was opened to North Conway. When the Portland & Ogdensburg reached Intervale in 1874, the PGF&C extended its trackage another 1.6 miles from North Conway to make the connection.

Before the resumption of construction in 1871, the town of Wolfeboro had attempted to have the line pass through before heading north. The PGF&C elected to follow a route avoiding hills, and Wolfeboro opened their own, independently financed, 12-mile branch in 1872.

North Conway's famous "Muscovite-inspired" depot was constructed in 1874. The 30 feet by 100 feet structure included an E. Howard eight day clock. The PGF&C also built a four-stall roundhouse, turntable, freight house, section car house, and numerous yard tracks.

PGF&C became part of the Eastern Railroad in 1878, and it in turn came under the control of the Boston & Maine in May 1884. During its most profitable period, the Conway Branch hosted some 28 freight and passenger trains daily. Commodities shipped south on the line included lumber and other forest products, farm products, and granite, while northbound trains returned with farm supplies, feed, and fuel. Passenger trains carried vacationers, "drummers" (traveling salesmen), children traveling between home and school, and—especially profitably—mail, newspapers, and express.

Ice became an important commodity on the line in the early years of the century, although by the 1920s both this and logging had begun to slip appreciably in volume. Gravel—in abundance in several locations on the Conway Branch—is actually what has kept the freight business alive on the line.

When skiing became an especially popular American pastime, the B&M realized the potential for profit and good public relations by running *Snow Trains*. These trains were very popular indeed; they included a dining car for the three-hour trip from Boston, a "Snow Train Service Shop" set up in the baggage car where one could buy sportswear and ski accessories, and rent skis, poles, snowshoes, and even toboggans. When the snow was good the trains ran in multiple sections to accommodate the crowds. In their heyday, *Snow Trains* originated in Rockport and Worcester as well as Boston.

Longtime B&M enthusiasts Dana D. Goodwin and H. Arnold Wilder describe one special occurence on a *Snow Train* making its way southward through Crawford Notch on the Maine Central:

...as the trains left Crawford Station and slowly made their way down around Mt. Willard to Willey Brook and Frankenstein Trestle, passengers were treated to a scenic spectacle of Nature's wonders, unscheduled and unrehearsed. The moon, probably about three quarters full, had risen above the top of Mt. Webster and reflected on all the shining snow and crevices of the Notch as we wound our way down, to the accompaniment of brakes applying and releasing and long lonesome whistle calls at ledges and bridges. Many of the coaches had their lights dimmed so that all might witness the splendor of it all; the timing of it which none could have anticipated. To a lessor

Train 2911, the Dover-Intervale local, arriving at Milton, New Hampshire at 11:56 a.m., on an overcast July 7, 1956. That's the crew of the way freight on the platform. Stanley W. Cook photo.

extent the same scene could be enjoyed down the Conway Branch past the Chocoruas and Ossipee Valleys. An added bonus for *Snow Train* devotees, to be long remembered[9].

Indeed, so dependable was this business that the B&M listed two similar, seasonal trains in its winter 1947 timetable. Train No. 2919, the *Skier*, left Boston on Fridays (with adjustments for Christmas and New Year's) at 5:50 p.m., between late December and mid-February. It was listed as a "Diesel Powered Train" carrying coaches (in 1948 it carried "Buffet Parlor Car 291 Boston to Intervale"). On subsequent Saturday mornings (in 1947 only) the *Eastern Slope* departed North Station at nine also with a diesel and coaches.

Neither train was advertised in the 1951 or 1952 timetables, but the *Skier* reappeared for the winters of 1953 through 1956. Unlike most trains for the Conway Branch, these typically ran express to Dover and skipped many of the usual local stops on the Branch. In 1956, the last year of the *Skier*, there were scheduled

two other weekday round-trips on the Branch, one on Sundays. The June 1958 timetable found a single daily round-trip, and this train, a single RDC, lasted into 1961, when it was finally dropped, ending nearly 100 years of regular passenger service. After that, only occasional excursion trains were sponsored on the Branch.

Another popular name was the *Mountaineer*, a summer sight-seeing train, which made a one-day round trip between Boston and Littleton & Bethlehem. Between 1944 and 1952 the train was covered by Unit 6000, affectionately referred to as the "Tin Fish." It left Boston at lunchtime and returned to the city in the late evening. In addition to the beauties of rural New Hampshire along the Conway Branch, the train passed through spectacular Crawford Notch on the Maine Central at about 4:00 PM northbound and 7:00 p.m. southbound.

The complete round trip made for a long day, but what a wonderfully picturesque ride it was. The view of vermilion and gold foliage of those Septembers was unsurpassed.

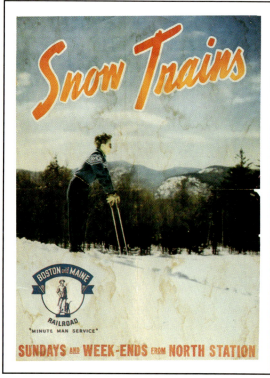

At left are three portraits of the Snow Train by Dick Hamilton from the collection of Dwight A. Smith. **Above left**: Busses are waiting to take skiers to the slopes as E-7 3810 swirls up loose snow at North Conway on February 14, 1954. **Center left**: B&M diner Birch provided riders with hearty fare for a day of skiing. **Below left**: The same train has departed for Intervale, leaving a platform of skiers. Both photos from January 17, 1954. **Top**: A 1950s B&M Snow Train poster from the author's collection. **Above right**: Russell F. Munroe rode the fantrip of February 29, 1964 and recorded this vivid North Conway depot scene. **Below right**: One year later, Richard W. Symmes made this photo of a March 1965 Railroad Enthusiasts' fantrip at Sanbornville. The train had to turn south at Mount Whittier because of an iced-over grade crossing.

Above: Rail service on the Wolfeboro Branch was a sometime thing as the years wore on. Russell F. Munroe photographed a local freight crossing Lake Wentworth on July 13, 1963.
Below left: Conway Depot, an attractive, typical B&M station, was sadly demolished to accommodate a highway improvement. Arthur E. Mitchell photo.
Below right: The roll sign for the Mountaineer shows the B&M sign painter's unique style.

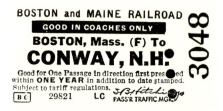

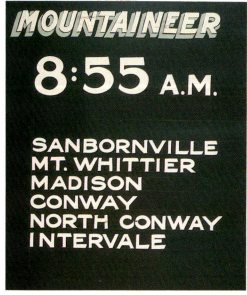

Above: North Conway's beautiful depot looks especially pleasant and inviting in this summer 1954 photograph by Arthur E. Mitchell. Moments later a GP-7 would couple onto the baggage car for the trip to Boston. *Below*: Sunrise greets the Conway Branch local, ID2, as it drifts into Ossipee on a colorful October 7, 1971. H. Bentley Crouch photo.

V

INTO THE WOODS

The New Hampshire Mainline

All set now, up through Converse we clack. The scenery is great in the sharp clear air. Then on through a place I always heard called "Gungawam"... To go through this territory on a cold, clear night was something! You could reach up and pick the stars right out of the sky, provided the Northern Lights didn't get in the way.

Ralph Fisher
Vanishing Markers

The Boston & Maine's New Hampshire Mainline has its origins in the Boston & Lowell Railroad (B&L), a successful New England carrier which operated 670 route-miles in three states at its peak. Passengers first rode on this route on June 24, 1835, when there were two round trips per day. Trains north to Concord were made possible by extensions of the Nashua & Lowell Railroad in 1838 and the Concord Railroad in 1842.

Through service from Concord to White River Junction began in 1848, with the completion of the Northern Railroad of New Hampshire. This road was leased to the Boston & Lowell in 1884, the B&L being leased to the Boston & Maine in June 1887. The Concord Railroad itself was leased to the B&M in 1895, thus bringing the complete Boston-White River Junction route under B&M control.

Of the several available routes available from Boston to Canada, this one became by far the most pro-

ductive and heavily traveled. The road was double tracked the 73 miles to Concord, facilitating the frequent and speedy movement of trains.

Dwight Smith—a B&M freight traffic representative during the fifties, and later the lauded founder of the Conway Scenic Railway—has written this interesting description of Enfield, 11 miles east of White River Junction, providing a nice grasp of detail for a typical rural station in 1952:

Enfield was a fairly busy station, with a dispatcher's wire for train orders, a Western Union wire, Railway Express Agency shipments, U.S. Mail, tickets, and baggage to handle as well as billing a daily carload of milk from H. P. Hood creamery located across the tracks from the depot.

Eight passenger trains passed Enfield every day, four in each direction between Boston and White River Junction. Four of the trains carried through cars and did not stop at Enfield. The other four passenger trains were all-stops locals. Three through freights in each direction also passed through Enfield every 24 hours. BU-1, BU-3, and 351X ran from Boston to White River Junction, with BU-1 usually handling empty milk cars as well as freight for the Canadian Pacific and Central Vermont. Southbound freights carried symbols UB-2 and JB-490. The third southbound was No. 352, primarily a train of loaded milk cars[10].

There is a timeless quality to a railroad track stretching off into the distance. This is the New Hampshire Mainline at Lebanon, New Hampshire in October 1961. RWJ photo.

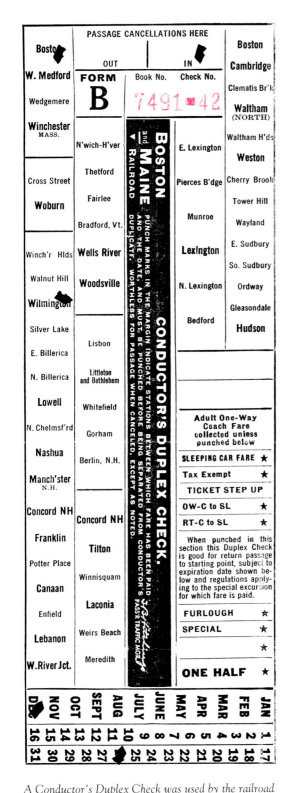

PASSAGE CANCELLATIONS HERE

OUT	IN

FORM B

Book No. — Check No.

7491 42

Boston		Boston
W. Medford		Cambridge
Wedgemere		Clematis Br'k
Winchester MASS.		Waltham (NORTH)
	N'wich-H'ver	Waltham H'ds
	Thetford	E. Lexington	Weston
Cross Street	Fairlee	Pierces B'dge	Cherry Brook
Woburn	Bradford, Vt.		Tower Hill
		Munroe	Wayland
Winch'r Hlds	Wells River	Lexington	E. Sudbury
Walnut Hill	Woodsville		So. Sudbury
Wilmington		N. Lexington	Ordway
Silver Lake		Bedford	Gleasondale
E. Billerica	Lisbon		Hudson
N. Billerica	Littleton and Bethlehem		
Lowell	Whitefield		
N. Chelmsf'rd	Gorham		Adult One-Way Coach Fare collected unless punched below
Nashua	Berlin, N.H.		
Manch'ster N.H.		SLEEPING CAR FARE ★	
Concord NH	Concord NH	Tax Exempt ★	
Franklin	Tilton	TICKET STEP UP	
Potter Place	Winnisquam	OW-C to SL ★	
Canaan	Laconia	RT-C to SL ★	
Enfield	Weirs Beach		
Lebanon	Meredith	When punched in this section this Duplex Check is good for return passage to starting point, subject to expiration date shown below and regulations applying to the special excursion for which fare is paid.	
W. River Jct.		FURLOUGH ★	
		SPECIAL ★	
		★	
		ONE HALF ★	

(vertical text center) **BOSTON and MAINE RAILROAD** · **DUPLICATE WORTHLESS FOR PASSAGE WHEN CANCELED, EXCEPT AS NOTED.** · **PUNCH MARKS IN THE MARGIN INDICATE STATIONS BETWEEN WHICH FARE HAS BEEN PAID AND THE DATE, AND MUST BE PUNCHED BEFORE BEING SEPARATED FROM CONDUCTOR'S PASS TRAFFIC MGR.** · **CONDUCTOR'S DUPLEX CHECK.**

DEC	NOV	OCT	SEPT	AUG	JULY	JUNE	MAY	APR	MAR	FEB	JAN
											17 1
					9	8	7	6	5	4	3 2 18
16	15	14	12	11 10	24	23	22	21	20	19	
31	30	29	28	27	25						

A Conductor's Duplex Check was used by the railroad as a receipt for cash-paying riders. Form B, in use in the 1960s, comprised all the stations on the New Hampshire Division, plus locations on the Central Mass and White Mountains lines as well. Author's collection.

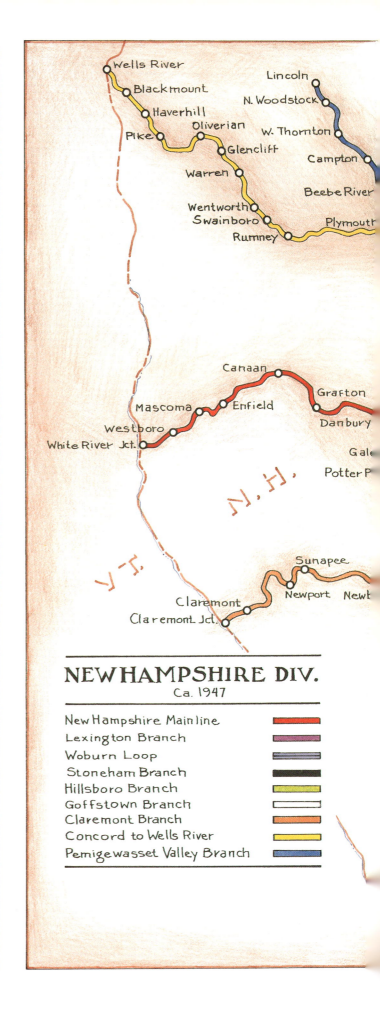

NEW HAMPSHIRE DIV.
Ca. 1947

New Hampshire Mainline	▭
Lexington Branch	▭
Woburn Loop	▭
Stoneham Branch	▭
Hillsboro Branch	▭
Goffstown Branch	▭
Claremont Branch	▭
Concord to Wells River	▭
Pemigewasset Valley Branch	▭

In addition to the through freights which Dwight Smith mentions (they were still running in 1962), the New Hampshire Mainline had local freights as well. In 1942, two locals worked the line north of Concord: one between Concord and Canaan three days a week, the other between White River Junction and Danbury six days. In 1954 one train worked between Concord and White River Junction on a two-day schedule. In 1962 this train worked south from the Junction to Stonehill, five days. On the lower part of the line a local worked from Boston to Lowell and return six days a week during the forties and fifties. In 1962 the schedule was Lowell-Stoneham, five days. Still another local appears in 1962, working five days Concord-Nashua and return. Milk trains on the New Hampshire mainline were an excellent source of income and continued into the early sixties.

The New Hampshire Mainline hosted on its rails some of the B&M's successful varnish. In 1947 the nightly *Red Wing - New Englander* carried three sleeping cars between Boston and Montreal, two via the Canadian Pacific and one via the Central Vermont and Canadian National, and it linked at White River Junction with the *Connecticut Yankee* from New York. The daily *Ambassador* carried a parlor car and a cafe grill car for the entire nine hour ride to Montreal. It connected at White River Junction with the *Day White Mountains* from New York. Also, two trains departing Boston at 9 a.m. and 4:30 p.m. made most local stops north of Lowell. The morning train became the *Alouette* in late 1954 when the line north of Plymouth was closed (see page 130).

The through sleeper on the *New Englander* was dropped in 1953, names were dropped from other trains in 1956, and other serious retrenchments in service came in June 1958 when the 3 a.m. and 11 a.m. trains were cut from the schedule. When the *Red Wing* disappeared after October 1959, just two daily trains were left. One was taken off very early in December 1961, and the last one survived until January 1965, when all passenger service north of Concord was ended.

When this last train of RDCs ceased operating, no longer could one ride north from Boston on a train for points in New Hampshire, Vermont, or Canada. Where a traveller could chose among three different routes to get to Montreal 15 years earlier, two of them with sleeping, dining, and parlor car service, now the only such trip to be taken was in one's memory .

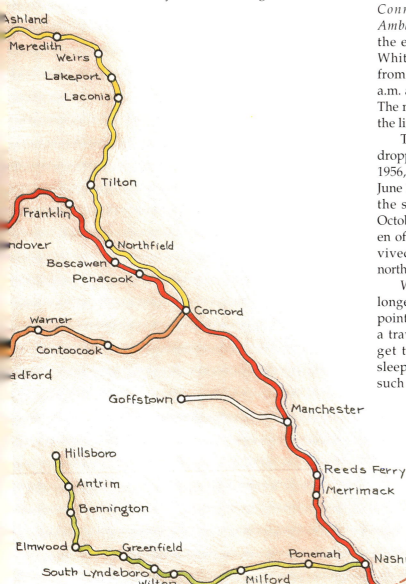

Left: The fireman is shoveling on the coal in B&M 2403, the last Consolidation in regular use, as the train picks up speed at Winchester for its brief run to Stoneham in July 1954. The old girl has a scant year left before scrapping. Superior photography by T. J. Donahue.

Below: This fine waterside scene is the work of Russell F. Munroe. F-2A 4257 is at Chelmsford in 1950.

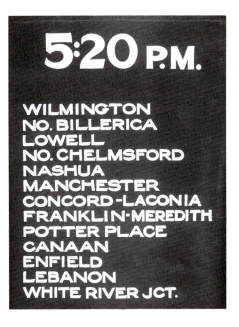

5:20 P.M.

WILMINGTON
NO. BILLERICA
LOWELL
NO. CHELMSFORD
NASHUA
MANCHESTER
CONCORD-LACONIA
FRANKLIN-MEREDITH
POTTER PLACE
CANAAN
ENFIELD
LEBANON
WHITE RIVER JCT.

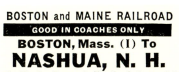

BOSTON and MAINE RAILROAD
GOOD IN COACHES ONLY
BOSTON, Mass. (I) To
NASHUA, N. H.
Good for One Passage in direction first presented
within ONE YEAR, addition to date stamped.
Subject to tariff regulations.
BC 20870   LC   PASS'R TRAFFIC MGR.   24112

Top left: The 5:20 p.m. roll sign for a train which will split into two parts at Concord—part for White River Junction and part for Laconia and Meredith. Such a schedule would indicate the last year or two of passenger service.

Top right: The early morning light finds the Red Wing-New Englander (*from Montreal to White River Junction via Canadian Pacific and Canadian National/Central Vermont, respectively, thence jointly to Boston*) at South Wilmington, bound for Boston in July 1950 behind the graceful proportions of E-8 3821. Too new for scrapping, she was sold to the Missouri Pacific in 1962 and ran ten more years. Donald G. Hills photo.

Center: A mid-day local arrives at North Billerica in the lens of Leon Onofri.

Bottom right: The imposing Nashua Union Station with an RDC the day before Christmas, 1959. As the letters below the former clock opening indicate, it was built by the Concord Railroad. Russell F. Munroe photo.

Into The Woods   113

Above: Because your author likes it so much, we reprise the oft published Donald G. Hills portrait of 3700 at Mascoma Lake on June 26, 1950. This is train 307 for Montreal via White River Junction.

Right: B&M 3715, the Kwasind, is southbound at Manchester on a sunny winter day with a mail train carrying considerable revenue. The end of the Postal contract in the mid-fifties spelled doom for dozens of marginal passenger trains in New England. David C. Bartlett photo.

Above: This is what White River Junction looked like before any of the trains arrived during the late afternoon rush in October 1961. Expectant employees are milling about, a handful of passengers is present, and if you look carefully, you can see a green eye on the CP target signal just to the right of the depot proper. RWJ photo. Below: Eight years later, on November 21, 1969, the power for train 3052, the night freight for Boston, idles in the background at the Westboro, New Hampshire yard. H. Bentley Crouch photo.

Into The Woods   115

THE LEXINGTON BRANCH

The Lexington & West Cambridge Railroad, opened in 1846 by the Fitchburg Railroad, ran from West Cambridge to Lexington Center. It broke its ties to the Fitchburg in 1857 and was purchased by the Boston & Lowell Railroad in 1869. The B&L then built a two-mile connection from its mainline at Somerville Junction to the L&WC just south of Lake Street, so that trains would enter Boston over B&L trackage. The first connection to the Fitchburg was then removed.

The north end of the line was extended when the Middlesex Central opened to Concord Center in August 1873, the trackage making a sharp turn to the west at Bedford. The B&L operated this under a lease. Further

augmentation came in 1885 when the B&L built north from Bedford—on the roadbed of an older, abandoned narrow gauge railroad—to its mainline in North Billerica.

At the time of World War II, freight service was handled by a local train going to North Billerica over the branch. By 1954 this local went even further north to Lowell, operating three days a week. A schedule for 1960 shows this train servicing the branch three days a week, that for 1961 five days, with the 1962 schedule returning to three days—interestingly, Monday, Tuesday, and Thursday. Business continued to dwindle, and by 1975 service was being provided by a local freight serving both the Lexington and the Central Mass Branches.

Passenger traffic on the Lexington Branch was always light beyond Bedford, and although there were 28 inbound trains on the branch in 1906, a mere three round trips to Bedford remained in 1933. Nonetheless, the relative paucity of trains did not mean that they were unimportant. On the contrary. We have George Dimond's memory of his childhood when

...the 4:31 p.m. out of Boston... carried the mail and arrived in Bedford at 5:14 p.m. The local contractor for the Post Office Department was always there to meet this train and rush the mail sacks to the Post Office in the center of Bedford, which was about a mile from the station. A large group of townspeople would gather at the Post Office and await the sorting of the mail which was usually completed well before the 6 p.m. closing time[11].

Business had increased again after the Second World War such that there were five weekday round trips to Bedford, four of them on a rush hour schedule. The 8:41 a.m. inbound and the 5:20 p.m. outbound were named *Patriot* and *Paul Revere*, respectively.

Two round trips were dropped in September 1949, the Saturday train in 1951, another round trip in 1955, and the penultimate in 1958. The final train lasted until January 1977. The *Patriot* name lasted into the spring of 1958, that of *Paul Revere* into the fall.

For a little branch having scant patronage, this one persevered with all the valor of Mr. Revere, himself.

*Below Left: Norton D. Clark made this dramatic photo of a Lexington commuter train at Route 128 with almost no light on January 28, 1955. Stanley Cook was responsible for preserving views of these two interesting stations on the branch, April 29, 1954. Just **below** is train 3211 at Lexington, 5:05 p.m., behind Mogul 1478 and bound for Bedford. At the **bottom** is Pacific 3630 on the point of train 3215, the Paul Revere, at North Lexington, 6:02 p.m.*

Above: Freight Extra 1451 has arrived at Bedford behind Mogul 1451 in the early fifties. Donald S. Robinson photo. **Below**: A handful of commuters awaits the morning Boston train at Pierces Bridge this biting, wintry 15th of February, 1955. Pacific 3625, after surviving 43 bitter winters, will succumb to the scrapper the following August 11. Norton D. Clark photo.

THE WOBURN LOOP

What was to become the Woburn Loop was opened in December, 1844 when the Boston & Lowell opened its first branch, 1.9 miles of track between the mainline at Winchester to Main Street, Woburn. Trackage back to the mainline at North Woburn Junction was opened by the B&L in November 1885.

Through the 1940s and 1950s the Loop experienced heavy passenger business. Often, trains for Wilmington and Lowell went this way because patronage was excellent. The Woburn Loop was double track for its entire length and was used by the Boston & Maine as an alternate main line. Thus it was not uncommon to encounter the occasional mainline varnish operating over the Loop. A single local freight worked the Loop six days a week in the fifties, reducing its activity to three days in the sixties.

The McGinnis administration closed the Loop north of Woburn Center in June 1959, tearing up the track in 1961 after 74 years of service. The beautiful and ornate Woburn station (except for its clock tower, virtually identical to the Marblehead depot) was demolished at this time, passengers being accommodated in a characterless aluminum shed south of the former depot. By 1981 the remaining track was in deplorable condition, long the victim of virtually no maintenance whatever dating from the mid 1950s, and service was ended by the MBTA in that year.

Top: The Woburn Loop was frequently used to divert trains around problems on the mainline; local train 302 from White River Junction usually ran via the mainline. Today 1801, one of three Canadian Pacific E-8s, is on the point. Donald G. Hills photo.

Right: A P2 Pacific is southbound for Boston just after leaving Woburn station in October 1953. Norton D. Clark photo.

120   Boston & Maine

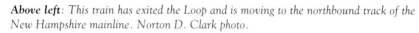

Above left: *This train has exited the Loop and is moving to the northbound track of the New Hampshire mainline. Norton D. Clark photo.*

Above center: *Wilmington to Boston train 3320 is approaching Eames Street crossing behind Pacific 3639. Donald G. Hills photo.*

Above right: *Pacific 3678 has a Boston bound train near Woburn in April 1952. Allan W. Styffe photo.*

Left: *The home signal tells us that we are at the southernmost part of the Loop at Winchester. A dramatic late-afternoon shot by T. J. Donahue.*

Below: *In the late afternoon of April 1, 1954, Stanley Cook made this picture of a Wilmington-bound train on the Loop. Train 3325 stops at Central Square with Mogul 1468.*

Into the Woods
THE STONEHAM BRANCH

This short, 2.4 mile line opened from the mainline of the Boston & Lowell Railroad in 1862. The B&L leased the nearly completed tracks from the builder later that year, and in 1870 purchased it outright for $50,000, a bargain price.

The line actually took considerable time aborning, acquiring three separate charters: 1847, 1851, and 1859. According to historian Walter E. Lenk, "In 1855 everyone expected the Stoneham Branch to enter Medford[12]." Nonetheless, the 1859 charter changed routes and the followed path went from Stoneham Village north to Farm Hill where it went west to its junction with the B&L at East Woburn (later called Montvale).

Stoneham Branch trains were originally combined with Woburn trains as far as Winchester, but Stoneham gained separate trains when the Woburn Loop was completed in 1885. Between 1912 and 1919 there were four weekday round trips; by 1947 there were only two; by 1952 just one—which stuck it out until May 18, 1958. This quiet little branch had the distinction of playing host to the B&M's last Consolidation, No. 2403.

Above: The crew turns Consolidation 2403 on the Armstrong Turntable at Stoneham in a ritual whose time had all but expired on June 3, 1954. The 2403 was by this time usually assigned to the lone daily round trip. Stanley W. Cook photo. *Below*: Business must have been pretty good for the single daily train, if the eight coaches are any indication. Russell F. Munroe made this picture on June 24, 1953.

Into the Woods
THE HILLSBORO BRANCH

In the rolling New Hampshire hills, Mogul 1402 with white flags flapping is on its way to Hillsboro with a local freight on June 10, 1951. Dana D. Goodwin photo/Courtesy of the Boston & Maine Railroad Historical Society.

...the Hillsboro Branch... we are on a line so little used that grass grows almost unchallenged between the rails... ours is an up-country branch shrunken and shriveled, forgotten by all but a handful of railroad men and shippers... A sunset line, this.

R. M. Neal
High Green and the Bark Peelers

This country branch, with its unusual oblique right turn in the remote location of Elmwood, New Hampshire, became known as the Hillsboro Branch after a washout in 1934 and the major flood of 1936 undermined bridges and washed away roadbeds. The B&M made the best of what was left without throwing money into major repairs. The result was the 1943 combining of trackage from Nashua west to Elmwood, and Elmwood north to Hillsboro. The B&M acquired some additional land at Elmwood in 1952 to build a new connection to the

Elmwood-Hillsboro segment, allowing the removal of much unnecessary trackage and several buildings.

When first built, the branches in this region carried considerable quantities of farm produce, milk, and poultry. Local farmers were dependent upon the rails.

Although chartered in 1844 to build west from Nashua all the way to the Connecticut River, the Wilton Railroad had only reached 11 miles to Milford by 1850. It managed another five miles to Wilton a year later. Another entity called the Peterboro Railroad (controlled by the Boston, Lowell & Nashua) constructed some 11 additional miles of track west to Greenfield in 1874. Yet another railroad, the Manchester & Keene, began construction in 1879 from Keene east, meeting the Peterboro at Greenfield. For economic and political reasons, this is as far as the M&K got; nonetheless there was now a complete line from Nashua to Keene.

A very busy junction was established at Elmwood near the center of the line, when an intersecting line was

Into The Woods 123

Above: Switcher 1129 leads train N-1 past young skaters at Milford, New Hampshire on January 4, 1975. Tom Travers photo. Above center: Here is that most beloved of New England institutions—the covered bridge. B&M Mogul 1488 is at Bennington, New Hampshire on August 19, 1949. Stephen R. Payne photo. Above right: Don Robinson *rode Passenger Extra 6127 north to Hillsboro, New Hampshire on May 4, 1968, where he photographed the Budd Cars through the covered bridge. Right: A Maine Central boxcar and a B&M caboose disappear into a fiesta of fall color at Bennington on October 1, 1976. Richard Story photo.*

built between Worcester and Contoocook. For a time after 1887, the Nashua & Keene Branch served as the Boston & Maine's Southern Division mainline. In 1895 the B&M leased the Concord & Montreal—a more direct route to the north—and the trackage was downgraded in status to the Keene Branch.

In R. M. Neal's appreciative B&M book, *High Green and the Bark Peelers*, we have a glimpse of branchline freight railroading quite unlike anything else in print. The Hillsboro local began at Lowell and spent a whole day working northbound, returning the following day (Another such train worked in the opposite direction).

As Mogul 1455 leads 12 cars and a "buggy," Neal describes what little business the line holds: at Wilton, sawdust and cardboard boxes from a lumber mill, and textile machinery from a nearby plant; cars from a grist mill at Greenfield; a paper mill at Bennington; and a children's playthings factory at Antrim. We are not left wanting for engaging detail:

At Milford we get rid of some L.C.L.—less than carload lot—freight. Conductor Tilton and Brakeman Sargent and [Head Brakeman] Savage are busy with hand trucks, trundling these little shipments out of the local or way car. [Fireman]

Buckley isn't required to help, but the day is hot and he knows the train crew will be perspiring, so he, too, helps with the unloading. I look at the boxes and crates and other goods in the local car.

A wheelbarrow is going to Hillsboro. Some gallon cans of Sears Roebuck paint are in transit to Antrim. We have two boxes of General Electric light bulbs, other boxes of Kleenex. A carton of crepe-paper Halloween cups from the C. A. Reed Company of Williamsport, Pennsylvania, is part of our freight. Plumber's equipment for John J. Carey is in one corner of the car. Near a door are cans of poultry feed. A box of Hallmark greeting cards is in the car. We are carrying garden hose, too. Spiegel's mail-order house at Chicago has given us a shipment of small furniture, crated. A Montgomery Ward canoe is another of our items.

When Neal's story was published in 1950, the Hillsboro local began at Lowell. By 1954 it departed from Nashua and made the six-times-per-week round trip in one day rather than two. Eight years later the train operated just five days.

The Hillsboro Branch lingers on today as the Milford & Bennington, a century old relic of another era.

Into the Woods

THE GOFFSTOWN BRANCH

Like its nearby cousin in Hillsboro, the eight mile Goffstown Branch received this, its new name, in March 1936 as a result of the disastrous floods which ravaged New England. Major portions of the former North Weare Branch right of way were washed out between Goffstown and Henniker Junction. The last 17 miles of the branch were thus abandoned.

This line had a most fascinating history. Though chartered to go west from Manchester as far as Claremont, the New Hampshire Central ran out of money after reaching Henniker in 1850. Alas, the line was a pawn caught up in the power struggle between two larger roads, one of whom indirectly took control and ripped out the last six miles of track from Henniker back to North Weare, thus neutralizing the possibility of the branch falling into the competitor's hands. When track

was finally relaid some 40 years later, political fighting between the Boston & Maine and the Concord & Montreal kept it from opening until 1893, despite vociferous local public demand for transportation.

Passenger service became a memory in 1936 with the severe flooding from the heavy winter storm. In its reincarnation as the Goffstown Branch, this short line handled a modest freight business. For many years the local freight working the Portsmouth Branch from Manchester also worked the Goffstown Branch three days a week, but in 1962 this arrangement was changed and Goffstown business was handled by the Concord-Nashua local.

The Goffstown Branch had the distinction of having one of the the last covered railroad bridges owned by the B&M, sadly destroyed by fire in August 1976.

Left: The raw, spectacular beauty of the Goffstown Branch is revealed here in April 1978, as a maroon GP-7 and a blue caboose move a car from the paper mill. Arthur Purchase photo/collection of J. Emmons Lancaster.

Right: The Goffstown covered bridge in a winter still life on December 4, 1971 by Russell F. Munroe.

Center: A brakeman and his red flag protect GP-7 1574 as it creeps out of the covered bridge and onto the grade crossing. The squaring of this end of the locomotive is a remnant of its days in passenger service when steam generators were installed in many B&M GPs.

Below: The short little freight has continued into town past the former passenger depot. Two photos from October 8, 1973 by Tom Travers.

THE CLAREMONT BRANCH

Chartered in 1848 to build to the town of Claremont on the Connecticut River, the Concord & Claremont Railroad completed the first 27 miles to Bradford in 1850. The Northern Railroad, from Concord to White River Junction, took control of the C&C in 1854 to prevent the possibility of its diverting through traffic. Construction did not begin again until 1870, but by 1872 the C&C finally reached Claremont.

From the years during World War II through 1954, the B&M operated a daily local freight from Claremont 23 miles east to Newbury, but from Newbury east there was no service at all. Samuel Pinsley bought the line from the B&M in 1954, naming it the Claremont & Concord Railway, and continued to operate freight, albeit on a diminishing basis.

Traversing this heavily wooded, 57 mile branch were two weekday round trip passenger trains in 1947, both of them based at the Claremont end. Already bus-es were appearing in the timetable to augment the schedule. On March 8, 1953, the evening round trip made its final run into Claremont Junction; this had been the only Sunday train as well. Left was one round trip based in Concord, departing 10:50 a.m. and arriving Claremont at 12:55 p.m. Its return began at 3:20 p.m., and it was back in Concord by 5:25 p.m. There were convenient connections at Concord with Boston trains.

This same schedule was continued by the Claremont & Concord when it took over in 1955 (for which they used a silver and red gas-electric car), but by the time of the October 30 timetable, a single bus round trip—provided by the Boston & Maine Transportation Company—had replaced rail service. Nelson Blount's *Steamtown* had its origins here in the summer of 1961, when for several weeks a steam train ran between Bradford and Sunapee, but conditions were not favorable and Blount sought a more receptive home for the operation at Keene on the Cheshire Branch.

The pretty line past Lake Sunapee had truly seen better days.

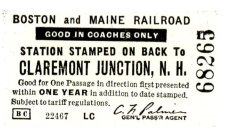

Above left: Contoocook Depot and its pretty covered bridge were once the site of a junction for a line which went all the way to Worcester. After the 1936 flood, said line terminated just a few miles south at Emerson. Donald G. Hills photo.

Below Left: John F. Kane happened across these three 44-tonners in this most photogenic of poses: Claremont & Concord 31, Hoosac Tunnel & Wilmington 16 (both of these roads properties of railroad entrepreneur Samuel Pinsly) and B&M 110.

Above Right: Dispatcher Preston Johnson made occasional trips on the B&M to see the lines and record with his camera. Today, January 22, 1953, he is riding in the cab of Mogul 1493 from Claremont Junction to Concord on train 3808, across sparkling sunlit landscapes of white snow. With a 25 minute layover in Concord, it's four hours, 15 minutes to Boston. Just in time for hot toddy!

Below Right: Four passengers from the just arrived Concord local are braving the cold until the southbound connection for Greenfield, New Haven, and points south is here in about 20 minutes, God willing. The conductor is walking to the depot to check in with the agent and the fireman is putting water in the tank. Photo made January 22, 1953 by Preston Johnson.

Into the Woods
BY LAKE WINNEPESAUKEE

Five years after the Northern Railroad opened its line from Concord to White River Junction, the Boston, Concord & Montreal Railroad in 1853 made its bid to control traffic to the northwest of Boston by completing its own line north from Concord. Its route passed through Laconia, alongside Lake Winnepesaukee at Lakeport, Weirs, and Meredith, and on to Plymouth and Woodsville, where it connected with the White Mountains Railroad and, just across the river, with the Connecticut & Passumpsic Rivers Railroad at Wells River (see Chapter VII). The Boston & Lowell leased the BC&M in 1884, and was in turn leased by the B&M in 1887.

The "Lakes Region" line, as it later appeared in timetables, was indeed one of the prettiest on the B&M system. Unfortunately, the 42 miles between Plymouth and Woodsville yielded scant freight revenue, and the line only survived into the early 1950s.

To get a feel for this territory, we join Dwight

Smith for a trip he took in a diesel cab on Saturday, October 11, 1953, a beautiful fall day.

The view from the fireman's seat of the 3809 was truly impressive, a much better vantage point than those dusty plush seats back in the coaches. Up through Tilton, Laconia, Lakeport, the Weirs, and Meredith we rolled. The tracks skirted the water's edge at many places as we traversed the heart of New Hampshire's lakes region. On up the grade to Ashland where a bustling woolen mill and a paper mill at the end of a steep spur furnished carload revenues to the B&M. Then to Plymouth, where the Pemigewasset Valley Branch diverged on its run to the paper mill town of Lincoln. Next we passed through the Baker River Valley villages of Rumney, Wentworth, and Warren.

Another grade up to Glencliff, where a sid-

We are at Weirs Beach on Lake Winnepesauke, this brilliant late afternoon in August 1953. Our train, the Alouette, has come down from Montreal and will be at Boston by 6:35 p.m. If we thought we might like to experience a leisurely sightseeing trip on the lake on the Mt. Washington, we would get off here. But seeing as how we are *somewhat tired from the many miles of gorgeous but enervating scenery, we shall repair to the CP open ended observation-lounge for a much needed martini in the presence of good New Hampshire pine tree air and the setting sun. Donald G. Hills photo.*

Above: *Summer-weekdays-only Plymouth to Concord local train 404 at The Weirs, New Hampshire, at 1:09 p.m. on July 5, 1952. If you had your choice, would you be on the train, one of the swimmers or picnicers, or cruising on the lake aboard the* Mount Washington? *Stanley W. Cook photo.*

Right: *Photographer Donald G. Hills was 17 miles up the line at Plymouth, five years earlier in 1947, where he photographed the activity at the engine-house there. At Plymouth was the junction with the branch into the Pemigewasset Valley.*

ing held cars of coal destined for the heating plant of the state sanitarium. Down through the many stations and sidings located within the township of Haverhill (i.e. Oliverian), Pike with an active bobbin mill, Haverhill itself with a small station located high on a hill above the village, Blackmount with its busy sidings serving creameries, lumber mills, feed stores, and a grocery warehouse. Then Horse Meadow, where a siding was used to spot cars of coal for the Grafton County Farm, and finally the busy yard and station at Woodsville itself.

At Woodsville the 3809 and a B&M RPO car were cut off, and glistening maroon and gray Canadian Pacific E-8 No. 1801 and a CP baggage mail car were attached to our train, now CP No. 211, but still the *Alouette*[13]...

The level of passenger service had been consistent since the Depression. It included the daytime *Alouette* between Boston and Montreal carrying a Canadian Pacific buffet parlor car, a connection north from Concord with the nighttime *Red Wing* from Boston, the weekday *Overnighter* from Boston to Woodsville carrying a through sleeper from New York's Grand Central Station, a daily local train between Concord and Woodsville connecting with the *Ambassador* at Concord (only these last two making the local stops between Plymouth and Woodsville), and one other weekday local between Concord and Plymouth connecting with the *Cannonball*.

After October 30, 1954, the B&M no longer offered service north of Plymouth, the 37 miles of track to Blackmount being removed shortly after. From this point, when there were three weekday round trips from

BOSTON and MAINE RAILROAD
GOOD IN COACHES ONLY
STATION STAMPED ON BACK TO —
WOODSVILLE, N.H.
Good for One Passage in direction first presented
within **ONE YEAR** in addition to date stamped.
Subject to tariff regulations. *S.B.Stitchings*
[B C]   4645   LC   PASS'R TRAFFIC MGR.
93837

BOSTON and MAINE RAILROAD
GOOD IN COACHES ONLY
LITTLETON and BETHLEHEM, N.H. To
HALF   FA
WOODSVILLE, N.H.
Good for One Half-Fare Passage in direction
first presented within **ONE YEAR** in additi
to date stamped.
Subject to tariff regulations. *S.B.Stitchings*
[B C]   29126   LC½   PASS'R TRAFFIC MGR.
253

Left: A great day, a fabulous train, and excellent depot action add up to make this quintessentially New England rail photograph. Stanley W. Cook was there at 3:47 p.m., Saturday, June 21, 1952, when train No. 9 arrived at Ashland, New Hampshire from Concord. The equipment is gas electric car 1140, the "Sacred Cow" (class DX-1b C-C, built by Ingersoll-Rand in 1935, 800 hp) and a trailer. They don't make them like this anymore!

Top: On January 3, 1972, John F. Kane and a colleague chased B&M freight C13 up this line by the lake and then up the branch to Lincoln. This is the first of two photographs of the train; the second is on page 137. We see GP-9 1718 and RS-3 1506 with its train at Lakeport, New Hampshire.

Above: B&M tickets were generally printed in black on an ivory stock. Half-fare tickets were printed in red. The agent selling the ticket stamped it with his dater-die which included the station name and date of sale. The ticket at left could be sold from any destination to Woodsville, while the one at right was specifically for passage between Littleton-Bethlehem and Woodsville. The latter variety was common whenever the volume of business demanded it.

Into The Woods   133

Boston, passenger service cuts were made repeatedly until 1959, the last year of Plymouth service. For several years, two daily, summer-only trains went as far as Meredith while fall-winter-spring trains terminated at Laconia. The trimming continued to January 1965 when all service was ended north of Concord.

Three different freight operations utilized the Concord-Plymouth line in the forties and fifties. A local freight began at White River Junction three days a week, with a trip to Wells River, Woodsville, and Plymouth where the crew put up for the night. After October 1954 this train operated six days a week from White River Junction, going only five miles south of Woodsville to end of track at Blackmount where it worked cars for First National Stores. A second local freight serviced Lakeport, Laconia, Tilton, and Franklin Falls six days a week (it worked to Plymouth on Saturdays in the sixties) with a B&M 44 ton diesel. The third train was the local freight to Lincoln, its chief duties being on the Pemigewasset Valley Branch (next section).

Noted B&M chronicler H. Arnold Wilder journeyed to Woodsville on the northbound *Alouette*, October 30, 1954, the last day of through passenger service on the line, to "record the end of an era":

...Train No. 20 from Montreal arrived and departed for the last time, headed by a big maroon CPR 1800-series E-8 diesel. Rain, somehow appropriately, began to fall as No. 24, on this night a two car train, (an RPO-baggage combine and a coach) behind E-7 diesel 3813, draped with black crepe, was made ready. At 5:20 p.m., under a barrage of torpedoes, we watched Woodsville station recede behind us for the last time; a meet with No. 409 at Oliverian, exchanges of good wishes among the crews, and one more wedge had been driven into the decline of a busy Mountain terminal.

H. Arnold Wilder
"Woodsville: A White Mountain Terminal"
B&M Bulletin

New England skies are often dark and gray, and yet landscapes under these conditions need not be dull. The richness of a cool, fall day, resplendent with subtle color, is revealed here at the Boston & Maine tracks just north of Tilton, New Hampshire in October, 1961. RWJ photo.

THE PEMIGEWASSET VALLEY

A Railroad Enthusiasts' trip brought these eight Budd RDCs—6131 in the lead—to the tip of the Pemigewasset Valley Branch at Lincoln this colorfully rich and intense fall day in 1971. Many B&M RDC ends were painted white when the blue logo was applied in the 1950s, but by this time logos were being applied directly onto a stainless steel surface. Stephen B. Horsley photo.

> *The winding Pemigewasset, overhung*
> *By beechen shadows, whitening down its rocks,*
> *Or lazily gliding through its intervales,*
> *From waving rye-fields sending up the gleam*
> *Of sunlit waters.*
>
> *Summer Saunterings by the B&L, 1886*

The "Pemi," as it has become affectionately known, was built primarily to tap the enormously lucrative lumber business in the woods adjoining the Pemigewasset River. Many of the towns along its path sprang up as logging towns as the business flourished.

The Boston, Concord & Montreal Railroad completed its northbound trackage as far north as Plymouth, New Hampshire in January 1850, making very fast transportation possible for eager travelers from, say, the Boston area. Resort business all through the Valley grew rapidly as coaches met passengers at Concord and carried them to popular establishments in Campton, Thornton, Woodstock, and in Franconia Notch itself, the Flume House and the Profile House. ("Profile" refers to "the Old Man in the Mountains," sometimes called the "Great Stone Face.")

The prevailing railroad fever struck here too, as it had all through New England, but events did not move so rapidly as elsewhere. Though a charter was granted in 1874 for a railroad to be built from Plymouth to Franconia, an unstable economic climate prevented construction until February 1882, when finally the economy rallied. Once started, the 20 mile line was quickly completed to North Woodstock in 13 months.

Above left: *For the bicentennial of the town of Lincoln, New Hampshire, in August 1964, we have on hand a festive crowd, four B&M RDCs, a switcher in the background, and the steamer from the East Branch & Lincoln—the logging railroad built by James E. Henry. Richard W. Symmes photo.*

Above right: *An inclement but lush June 28, 1968 finds a B&M high-rail truck at Thornton, New Hampshire, preceding the local freight (train O-4, whose headlight is seen in the distance) because the condition of the track had been permitted to deteriorate dramatically in the face of waning business. Donald S. Robinson photo.*

Eleven more miles of construction through the Notch would have connected the trains with a narrow gauge line on the northern side, but the Boston, Concord & Montreal was prudent enough to see the very minimal gains. All but one of the resort hotels already enjoyed rail service, the engineering work through the Notch—over a substantial grade—would have been very expensive, and several conservationist organizations were becoming increasingly vocal about all the serious damage being wrought by the lumbering business. Indeed, similarly minded citizens prevented the completion of Interstate Highway 93 through the Notch until 1988, and even now it is one of only a few sections of Interstate Highway in the United States just *two lanes wide*. This is is obviously a very proud tradition of the local populace, and one to be admired.

One additional mile was added about 1883 when lumber baron James E. Henry acquired thousands of acres of timberland in the watershed of the East Branch of the Pemigewasset River, establishing a thriving settlement which became the village of Lincoln.

In the early years of the branch, four round trip passenger trains provided daily service. From about 1900 through the Depression there were three such trips, while in April, 1934 service (via gas car) was reduced to two. The automobile, in its furious onslaught in these years, was directly responsible for the opening up of this region to major tourism. When the great New England

Hurricane of September 21, 1938 inflicted massive damage to the line, the Boston & Maine gave up on scheduled passenger service.

The railroad had tried a Sunday schedule for skiers in the last winter of regular passenger service, 1937-38, and Snow Trains also ran occasionally from this time until a few years after World War II.

Freight movement was reduced considerably in the 1930s with the declining lumber business. After World War II only three lumber mills were still operating, and the one remaining logging railroad, the East Branch & Lincoln, closed in 1950, although successor companies did employ an ex Grasse River diesel for yard switching. The Franconia Paper Company in Lincoln provided sufficient business through the fifties and sixties that daily service was provided by two locals working in opposite directions, the crews laying over in Lincoln. Later the crews switched trains at Lakeport so that each could return to home base daily. In 1968 service was reduced to three round trips per week. The paper mill closed in 1970 because of anti-pollution regulations, was opened again intermittently under several different managements, and ultimately closed for good. The State of New Hampshire bought the branch during the mid seventies, and it is now the home of two tourist railroads, the Winnepesauke Railroad and the Hobo Railroad.

Above: Freight C-13 is on its way to the Pemi, and is seen here north-bound crossing the Ashland Bridge. Another shot of this train is on page 133. John F. Kane photo.

Below: And here is proof that the sun does sometimes shine on the Pemi. GP-7 1569 is hitched to the mill steam line in February 1961. Note the still-in-use water tower. Joseph R. Snopek collection.

I knew when I first saw this photograph of the East Deerfield Yard that I wanted to give it a place of prominence, because it is such an atypical view of this strategic location. Unfortunately, the whereabouts of the original photographer were not known, and it was only after considerable detective work that he was located.
Edgar A. Swift photo/John F. Kane collection.

VI

THROUGH THE BERKSHIRES
The Fitchburg Division

The men on the Fitchburg Division are different, the other railroaders say; they're harder, tougher. They need to be. Following the Deerfield River up from Greenfield into the mountains, the tracks are set in a graceful beauty that has thrilled hundreds of photographers... But in winter the wind shrills down the gap in the hills, snow cuts like a thousand tiny knives against a man's face, and a flagman who must plod back a half mile to protect his train will be stiff with cold before he returns to the buggy and its warmth. A man must be durable to work in winter on the Fitchburg.

R. M. Neal
High Green and the Bark Peelers

The Boston & Maine's Fitchburg Division, the route over which the vast majority of its mainline freight tonnage passed, was a major source of revenue for the railroad throughout its history. The existence of the Hoosac Tunnel gave the B&M a significant advantage over its rival, the Boston & Albany, in its ability to move freight in and out of New England.

The Fitchburg Division began in 1839 as the 1.5 mile Charlestown Branch Railroad, intended to bring freight from the Boston & Lowell at East Cambridge to Swett's Wharf in Charlestown. In 1841 another four miles of trackage were built to West Cambridge to serve icehouse sidings to Fresh and Spy Ponds. Major expansion came in March 1845 when the Fitchburg Railroad Company completed construction of its new line from West Cambridge to Fitchburg, some 45 miles.

By 1850, another company—the Vermont & Massachusetts Railroad, sharing the same backers as the Fitchburg Railroad—had completed its line from Fitchburg west to Greenfield, 105 miles from Boston. The similarly incorporated Troy & Greenfield would provide service west as far as Williamstown, with two other small carriers filling in the gap to Troy: the seven-mile Vermont Southern and the 34-mile Troy & Boston. Sadly, 25 years would pass before through service could be inaugurated because of the long, expensive and sometimes fatal construction project to build a five-mile tunnel through Hoosac ("Forbidden") Mountain. Not until February 9, 1875 was the line completed through the tunnel. The project had taken 23 years, and consumed $20 million and 195 lives.

During the year prior to completion, the Fitchburg Railroad leased the smaller lines and thus ran the eventual through service from Boston to Troy under its own name.

Yet another railroad—the Boston, Hoosac Tunnel & Western—began operations to the Erie Canal (at a location eventually to be named Rotterdam Junction) in 1879. Even though it carried "Boston" in its title, its trackage actually began at the Vermont-Massachusetts state line on the Fitchburg Railroad, paralleling it some 20 miles to Johnsonville, New York, and crossing it *four* times in this short span. From Johnsonville it went west across the Hudson to Mechanicville and beyond. The Fitchburg took control of the BHT&W in 1887.

On July 1, 1900, the Boston & Maine leased the Fitchburg Railroad, vastly expanding the size of the system. Thirteen years later it would add the last 8.7 miles, between Dole Junction and Brattleboro, making the B&M as large as it would ever be, 3,269 miles controlled and operated.

After World War II, when the B&M invested significant sums in upgrading its passenger equipment for trains into Maine—its busiest corridor—the trains to Troy did not share in these amenities. Any profits realized from Fitchburg Division through passenger trains were the result of U.S. Mail contracts and other head-end business. Troy-bound trains were just not in great demand. That a passenger could connect to Albany didn't really help; one had to wait both in Troy and again in Albany before traveling west. The Boston & Albany had direct service with convenient Chicago connections. And so none of the B&M's new streamlined coaches ever went to Troy.

The *Minute Man* carried a parlor restaurant car to Troy and a Pullman sleeper destined to Chicago (dropped around 1949). Taking five hours, 15 minutes, Boston to Troy, it was considerably faster than the four other weekday trains to Troy which took between six and a half and seven hours with all their local stops. They had no on-board food, either. The *Minute Man* utilized Unit 6000 between April 1952 and December 1956, and this equipment did include a buffet service. In 1952 train No. 55, formerly *The Berkshire*, was assigned a "Budd Highliner" for the Boston to Troy run, vastly improving the comfort level of this non-food train. Stops were reduced from 25 to 18, and a 35 minute layover at Greenfield was eliminated. These improvements, plus the Budd equipment's ability to accelerate quickly, shaved nearly an hour and a half off the previous schedule.

Like so many of its sister routes of the B&M, the Fitchburg was surrounded by breathtaking views, especially west of Greenfield into the Berkshires where there were long, uninterrupted sections of unrelenting beauty.

Of the heavy freight tonnage traveling this double-track, east-west main, some 60 percent went in or out of Boston, the balance travelling between Mechanicville and Rigby, where traffic was interchanged with the Maine Central, a railroad blessed with some ten lines into Maine and two into New Hampshire and Vermont. In addition, the MEC interchanged at Northern Maine Junction with the Bangor & Aroostook, where untold quantities of potatoes and paper were disgorged annually and shipped all over America.

Such freight was brought to the Fitchburg from the Portland Division by way of three contiguous sections of track: Eight miles from Lowell Junction on the Portland Division to Lowell on the New Hampshire Division; Three miles from Lowell to North Chelmsford on the New Hampshire Division; and 13 miles from North Chelmsford to Ayer, the "Stony Brook" Branch.

With the intersection of the Connecticut River Line at Greenfield—and its important links north and south, it was inevitable that a major classification yard be established there. This came to happen at East Deerfield, a beautiful rolling Valley at the confluence of the Deerfield, Green, and Connecticut Rivers.

The following list provides the freight train symbol, city and time of departure, and train name for 1954 mainline freights:

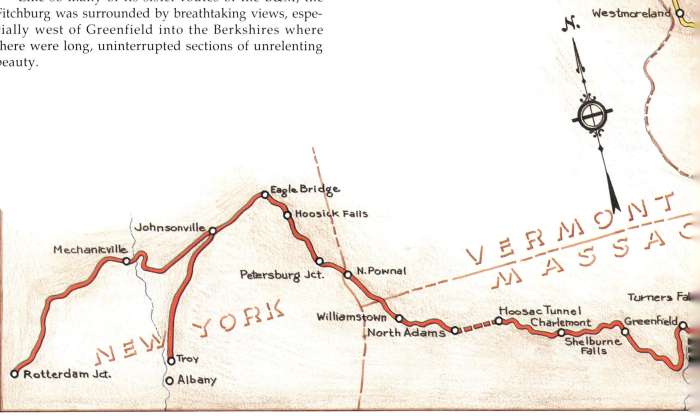

1954 Scheduled Mainline Freights

No.	From	To	Departs	Name
BM3	Bstn	M'Vle	6:30 p.m.	*The Big Chief*
MB2	M'Vle	Bstn	8:00 a.m.	*The Pathfinder*
BM11	Bstn	M'Vle	2:00 p.m.	
MB6	M'Vle	Bstn	6:30 p.m.	*The Hubber*
BR1	Bstn	Rtdm J	10:00 p.m.	
RB2	Rtdm J	Bstn	11:30 p.m.	*New Englander*
BR3	Bstn	Rtdm J	4:30 a.m.	
RB4	Rtdm J	Bstn	11:00 a.m.	*The Champion*
PM1	Ptlnd	M'Vle	12:30 a.m.	*The Clipper*
MP2	M'Vle	Ptlnd	10:00 a.m.	*The Forest City*
PM3	Ptlnd	M'Vle	7:00 a.m.	
MP4	M'Vle	Ptlnd	4:00 p.m.	
SM1	Sprfld	M'Vle	6:15 p.m.	
MS2	M'Vle	Sprfld	10:00 p.m.	
WM1	Wstr	M'Vle	6:00 p.m.	*The Westerner*
MW2	M'Vle	Wstr	9:00 p.m.	*The Night Hawk*

Bstn: Boston — M'vle: Mechanicville — Ptlnd: Portland — Rtdm: Rotterdam Junction — Sprfld: Springfield — Wstr: Worcester

Happily, this same level of activity was still shown in the 1962 schedule. The Fitchburg was holding its own for the B&M.

The local freight picture on the Fitchburg was also very healthy in 1952:

From	To	Frequency
Fitchburg	Ayer-Greenfield	6 days
Fitchburg	East Deerfield	6 days
Fitchburg	South Ashburnham	5 days
East Deerfield	East Fitchburg	6 days
East Deerfield	Gardner	6 days
East Deerfield	Hoosick	5 days
Troy	Mechanicville	6 days
Mechanicville	North Bennington	5 days

Except for the last two locals, which were combined when activity at Troy was downgraded considerably in the late fifties, the level of local freight remained very healthy well into the sixties on the Fitchburg.

As long as passenger service was frequent, the railroad made an attempt to provide connections at Greenfield between Fitchburg Division trains and those of the Connecticut River Line. One can see how helpful it would be for someone living some distance west of

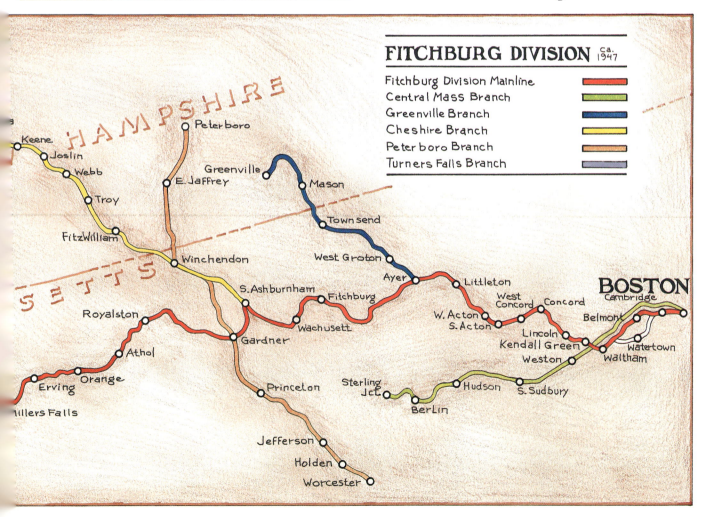

Boston to go first to Greenfield and then south to New York, rather than going east to Boston first and then south on the New Haven. But passenger service on the Fitchburg lost out quickly after the cancellation of the mail contract. It was truncated at Williamstown on January 19, 1958 and by December 30 service was further cut back to Greenfield. By April 23, 1960 all service stopped at Fitchburg.

Above left: RS-3 1540 appears to have battled some snowbanks with its commuter train this March 20, 1956, as it passes Waltham Depot. Norton D. Clark photo.

Below left: Circus trains have been a regular staple of B&M business for many years. The World of Mirth extra speeds past Belmont Depot on June 23, 1957 behind RS-3s 1540 and 1535. Russell F. Munroe photo.

Right: Color photographs of steam pushers are especially rare. This fine view taken at Waverly, Massachusetts in 1942 is by Donald S. Robinson.

Below right: The famous Unit 6000, here running as the Minute Man, has just passed under the Route 128 bridge in Weston on its return from Troy to Boston. In December the train would again run as the Cheshire, its final, short assignment before retirement. Russell F. Munroe photo.

Above left: Ayer, Massachusetts was a major junction point on the railroad. In this view we see a sharp, clean "Bluebird"—GP-9 1740, with a westbound freight, the tower and its order board, and Ayer Depot—with possibly the largest station roof known to man. John F. Kane photo.

Below left: Train 5507 for Troy, New York, is at West Concord, Massachusetts, heavy with mail and head-end revenue behind P4 Pacific 3711. Donald G. Hills photo.

Above: The tower clock tells us it's ten minutes to three this 1953 winter afternoon. A crisp, shiny looking RDC awaits a return to Boston here at the starkly handsome Fitchburg Depot. John F. Kane photo.

Below: Compared to the turmoil which would later embroil them, the 1952 campaign must have eventually seemed like a time of relative innocence for Pat and Richard Nixon. Longtime B&M train watcher Dana Goodwin recorded the campaign train at Fitchburg this bright day in May 1952. Courtesy Boston & Maine Railroad Historical Society.

Left: A work train was the only visible equipment at East Deerfield when Jack Armstrong made this photo on September 17, 1973.

Below, far left: Many photographers have made pictures from the "railfan bridge;" Wayne D. Allen made this fascinating night shot December 18, 1979.

Below, near left: We're talking thick foliage here on the Turners Falls Branch. Jack Armstrong photographed local E-5 on October 4, 1974.

Right: Richard Story went right down into the yard to take this picture, a brave act which one could not get away with today.

Below: Four beautiful GP-9s haul a train across the Deerfield River on an overcast October day in 1970. Stephen B. Horsley photo.

Above: A cold, clear morning—February 14, 1963. The stately Millers Falls Depot used jointly by the Boston & Maine and the Central Vermont lies mortally pierced after a freight wreck several days earlier. The obliterated track will be replaced but the building will have to be torn down. *Below*: Three days later, a much happier scene: GP-7s 1574 and 1575 and RS-3 1516 are at Deerfield with a long revenue freight. Two photos, Russell F. Munroe.

Above: F7 4265 is coming through and the snow is flying at Deerfield in February, 1969. Stephen B. Horsley photo.
Below: With nothing but red showing on the signal bridge ahead, photographer H. Bentley Crouch and the freight behind him—PB-2—are waiting at the end of double track at Soapstone, Massachusetts for train RM-1 to clear. Soon, out of the gloom comes GP-9 1723 on the point. In a minute, PB-2 will have a high green.

Above left: The Depot at Charlemont was yet another fine old station, and it, too, is sadly gone today. Richard W. Symmes was there October 24, 1965 to photograph this eastbound freight.

Below left: Now here is railroad art! Did you ever see such a glorious portrait of a work train? Photographed by the talented H. Bentley Crouch.

Above: On a beautiful, sunny May 30, 1954, Norton D. Clark and three army buddies visited the mouth of the Hoosac Tunnel, where they photographed a westbound freight with an A-B-B-A set of FTs headed by 4213. Note the multi-bulbed headlight.

Right: It's raining lightly at the Hoosac Tunnel east portal and FT 4212 has arrived with a westbound freight this fall day in 1950. We know by the high green that the eastbound iron is hot. Russell F. Munroe photo.

Above: "Bluebird" 1745 emerges from the east portal of the Hoosac Tunnel into a snowfall in March 1966. The metal work at the right of the locomotive is a remnant of the catenary system which disappeared with the coming of diesels to the B&M in the early 1940s. Richard W. Symmes photo. **Below**: In addition to the baroque intricacies of the North Adams Depot, this photo shows the former catenary system which began here and stretched east some five miles through the Hoosac Tunnel. Donald G. Hills photo.

Above right: Enjoy this photograph, good colleagues, because there aren't many like it in color. Electric boxcab 5004 and two brothers are about to pull a steam freight through the Hoosac Tunnel. These electrics were introduced in 1911 while the railroad was under New Haven control. You can thank Norton D. Clark for this 1941 photo. **Below right**: Three decades later, BM-7, behind Penn-Central power, is passing a B&M rail train at North Adams. It's not often that one sees B&M equipment in chrome yellow. Jack Armstrong photo.

Above: January 19, 1958 was the last day of B&M passenger service to Troy, New York, and E-7 3814 is about to take its train to Boston. This is the third paint scheme for this patrician beauty, and she was the only one of the 21 E-7s to be so painted.

Below: Crew members are conferring just prior to a run from Mechanicville in 1948. FT 4219 A&B are in their original paint scheme with the wings on the side instead of the Minute Man logo on the nose. Two photos, Norton D. Clark.

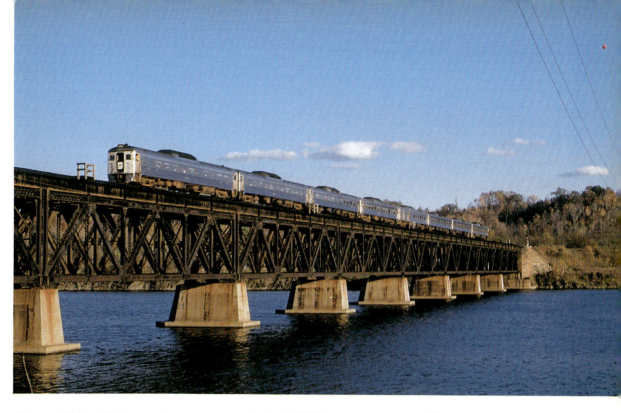

Above: A Railroad Enthusiasts' excursion train of eight Budd RDCs is crossing the deep blue waters of the Hudson River in October 1964. Note the RDC-3 in the middle. Jim Shaughnessy photo. **Below**: It's 6:10 p.m. on May 5, 1956 and E-7 3815 leads train 66 out of Troy, New York for Boston under a covered bridge built in 1885 and destroyed by fire in 1963. The head-end business looks good. Charles G. Parsons photo/William P. Nixon collection.

Through the Berkshires   155

THE CENTRAL MASS

The Central Massachusetts branch of the Boston & Maine is a typical example of the overbuilding which took place in the 1800s in New England. Every town wanted rail service, and there are literally hundreds of cases on record where business sense was thrown to the wind and hefty financial resources committed to building unneeded trackage. It seems to be a corollary that the less needed a line was, the more bucolic its scenery and the more quaint its stations. All too often the backers ignored the realities of too little potential for freight and passenger revenue. The Central Mass, as so many like it, went nowhere and passed through tiny hamlets

in so doing. While in retrospect we can deride the wasted money, we can surely revel in the breathtaking beauty of many of these lines.

The Massachusetts Central Railroad opened in 1881 from North Cambridge to Hudson (Oct. 1) and Jefferson's (Dec. 29), having reached an agreement with the Boston & Lowell to get its trains from North Cambridge into Boston. Shut down because of financial difficulties in 1883, the line was rescued by the Boston & Lowell which assumed control and reopened the line in 1885.

The B&L pushed the line westward with additional construction, reaching Northampton on the Connecticut

River in 1887 where it connected with the New Haven. When the Boston & Maine took control of the Boston & Lowell in June 1887, the Central Massachusetts Branch was part of the transaction. At the time the Central Mass was first constructed in 1881, it crossed a branch of the Fitchburg Railroad (from South Acton to Hudson and Marlboro, opened 1850) at Gleason Junction. While the Fitchburg extended this line south to Marlboro in 1855, it wasn't until 1903 that the Gleason Junction diamond was augmented with connecting trackage to facilitate the passage of Boston & Maine trains between Boston and Marlboro. The Central Mass became even more useful to the B&M passenger services when, in 1903, the creation of the Wachusett Reservoir and the subsequent track relocation over the now famous trestle bridge permitted trains to run to Clinton and Lancaster over the B&M's Worcester, Nashua, and Portland Main Line.

In the years surrounding the turn of the century, passenger business was actually quite robust, with fourteen inbound trains: four from Northampton, one from Lancaster, two from Clinton, five from Marlboro, and two from Wayland. But this level of activity did not last past World War I. The automobile made enormous inroads into the railroad business between the two wars. Northampton and Marlboro lost all passenger service on these tracks.

The B&M bisected the Central Mass in June 1938 for financial reasons, placing out of service the nine miles from Oakdale west to Rutland. It was a prophetic move, for on September 21 New England was devastated by a monster hurricane. The Central Mass was badly damaged.

Freight service on the east end was handled by a daily-except-Sunday round trip to Clinton Junction, including a jog to Marlboro, prior to World War II. The U.S. Government opened an ammunition depot just east of Ordway in 1942, and for the next three years the branch was nearly overwhelmed with movements there, often at night. After the war, the local freight rarely went beyond Berlin.

A 1951-52 grade separation project on the Fitchburg Division facilitated the elimination of four miles of adjacent, parallel track on the Central Mass track between Fens and Clematis Brook. Afterwards, Central Mass trains used the Fitchburg as far as Clematis Brook. At this time the local freight worked the branch three days a week. Business had improved so that 1960 saw daily weekday service. The 1962 schedule saw the freight going only as far as South Sudbury Monday-Wednesday-Friday, working through to Hudson and Marlboro Tuesday and Thursday. Freight patronage

The Clinton viaduct was built in 1903, a spindly but sturdy study in railroad design. Mogul 1455 is pulling a passenger train to Boston this brilliantly green May 18, 1955. What a splendid setting for a train! Norton D. Clark photo.

declined further and by 1975 the Central Mass shared its local freight with the Lexington Branch, with Hudson serviced once or twice a week.

The fall 1947 passenger timetable shows one and a half round trips from Lancaster and two and a half from Clinton. Post-War ridership declines were beginning to be serious by 1950, and Lancaster lost its service when trains were cut back to Clinton. Service from 1951 through 1957 was basically constant with four Boston-Clinton round trips, one of these being cut back to Hudson

in April 1955. The final steam run from Clinton to Boston took place on May 5, 1956. In recognition of the event's significance, the fireman of Train 3106 threw his shovel into the water at Boston's Drawbridge No. 1 as they passed. More cut-backs were made in 1958 and again in 1959, when only a single round trip remained. In 1965 the MBTA curtailed this service back to South Sudbury. The last passenger train left the branch in November 1971, a victim of deteriorating track and diminishing revenue.

Left: A day's work in Boston is done. Commuters are alighting at Waltham Highlands from train 3117 at 6:16 p.m., May 19, 1953. Stanley W. Cook photo.

Right: The roll sign for the 5:35 p.m. local to Clinton which included four flag stops.

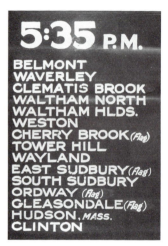

5:35 P.M.
BELMONT
WAVERLEY
CLEMATIS BROOK
WALTHAM NORTH
WALTHAM HLDS.
WESTON
CHERRY BROOK (Flag)
TOWER HILL
WAYLAND
EAST SUDBURY (Flag)
SOUTH SUDBURY
ORDWAY (Flag)
GLEASONDALE (Flag)
HUDSON, MASS.
CLINTON

The B&M experimented with an anti-accident grade crossing device in the late 1940s. At the approach of a train, it rose up from the street, flashing red, and reportedly broke axles on those occasions when motorists ignored it. Nonetheless, it successfully prevented rail-highway collisions. Donald S. Robinson photo made at Wayland, Massachusetts in July 1947.

BOSTON and MAINE R. R.

COUPON **12 RIDE** F
OF **TICKET**

GOOD FOR ONE RIDE BETWEEN
BOSTON, Mass. and

**MUNROE, WALNUT HILL
or WALTHAM HIGHLANDS**

Subject to tariff regulations.

12 R **01436** J.B.Stickney
PASS'R TRAFFIC MGR.

Far left: *Postcard collectors may recognize this famous Norton D. Clark photograph of B&M 2731 on the point of a local freight at Wayland, Massachusetts in 1947. The crew apparently appreciates this opportunity for immortality.*

Below: *Here is a way of life almost totally forgotten today—the crossing tender and his shanty. Time was when there were thousands of such facilities at grade crossings all across America. Train 3109 is behind Mogul 1455 at Waltham Highlands. Donald S. Robinson photo.*

Right: Gas cars were well suited for the passenger service requirements of the Central Mass Branch. Gas Car 187 rounds a bend on a golden April 9, 1955 with its trailer.

Below: The earth is greening this warm spring day, May 5, 1955, and Mogul 1493 is at Waltham Highlands with a commuter local. Two photos, Norton D. Clark.

Above: Well, you can see why they're called steamers. Mogul 1455 pulls through Wayland this wintry but bright March 31, 1956, the last year of steam on the railroad. Norton D. Clark photo.

Below: The Boston & Maine crossed the New Haven at South Sudbury, and—with the ornate depot, the manual interlocking semaphores, an order board, anxious passengers, and a quartet of vintage automobiles— Donald S. Robinson has created quite a colorful photograph. Train 3104 arrives behind Mogul 1402 for Boston early one morning in 1946.

Above: Local freights don't get much shorter; this one behind switcher 1227 is at Tower Hill on January 5, 1966.

Below: It almost seems as if the ground cover is on fire as Mogul 1495 comes steaming round the bend at Weston in February 1955. Two photos, Norton D. Clark.

Above: *During the summer of 1971, an ad hoc committee of citizens and politicians prevailed upon the MBTA to continue passenger trains on the Central Mass Branch, after the subsidy to operate this service had been deleted from the MBTA budget. Amazingly enough, the MBTA not only agreed to maintain the service but to add three round trips on a 60-day trial period. The experiment met with limited acceptance and the additional service was dropped on October 29, 1971. On the last day, train 737 heads west through Weston amidst brilliant late autumn foliage. H. Bentley Crouch photo.* **Below**: *The smoke is all black as freight K-8 passes into the distance with a local freight at Kendall Green on November 11, 1951. Preston S. Johnson photo.*

THE GREENVILLE BRANCH

The Fitchburg Railroad was the behind-the-scenes sponsor in the building of the Peterboro & Shirley Railroad to Greenville, New Hampshire, a line undertaken to offset the probable competition from the Nashua & Lowell system. The Fitchburg leased the P&S in 1847 with hopes of building on to Peterboro, where access would have been provided north to Concord and northwest to Vermont, but a disastrous business climate in the 1850s prevented any further progress beyond Greenville. By the time economic conditions rallied, other routes were firmly established. Thus this would-be important commerce link spent its life as an obscure freight branch.

A farmer's market and a grain mill at Greenville were two of the more productive customers on the branch. In the fifties a local freight worked the line six days a week; in the sixties business was such that Tuesday and Friday service was sufficient.

So little used was the branch, and so out of the way, that hardly anyone ever spoke of it. Imagine the surprise and pleasure of those riding a 1952 excursion fantrip as the beauties of the line revealed themselves.

Far left: The Greenville Branch turned sharply from the mainline at Ayer; the roofs of both the tower and station can be seen behind the C&O boxcar. Mogul 1460 is hauling freight away from the junction on February 8, 1951. Stephen R. Payne photo.

Near left: Passenger extra 1484 west, a 1952 excursion on the Greenville Branch, pauses for photos on the famous trestle near the northern end of the branch. Donald S. Robinson photo.

Top: In January 1978 the snowplow of this all-blue, westbound train derailed at West Groton, just a few minutes after the photographer and a friend vacated the soon-to-be point of impact for a better photo location on this side of the tracks.

Above: Local freight AY-1 is at West Groton, Massachusetts in June 1972, bound for Ayer. The close proximity of the track to the old colonial homes is characteristic of some New England branch lines. Two photos, Walter S. Kowal.

THE CHESHIRE BRANCH

The route of the Boston & Maine which leaves the Fitchburg Division main line at South Ashburnham and proceeds northwest, until it intersects the Connecticut River Line at Bellows Falls, is known as the Cheshire Branch. It began as the Cheshire Railroad, chartered in 1844, started in 1847, and reaching Keene in 1848. The road was constructed by unruly Irish workmen who drank and brawled frequently. The worst such incident occurred during the strenuous cutting of the summit west of Keene, when a man was killed and the Keene Light Infantry was called in. Nonetheless, the road was completed to Bellows Falls in January 1849. There it connected with the Sullivan Railroad to White River Junction. Connection to Montreal was achieved via the Vermont Central, the Vermont & Canada, and two other Canadian lines. The Cheshire Railroad was merged into the Fitchburg in 1890, the latter leased by the B&M in 1900.

Although it was part of the first through route to Montreal, it was soon overshadowed by the two others which eventually became known as the Canadian National and Canadian Pacific routes. Still, the Cheshire Branch played host to several name trains during the late 1940s: *Cheshire*, *Green Mountain Flyer*, *Monadnock*, and *Mount Royal*. The level of service was dropping fast because of increasingly low ridership; the *Green Mountain Flyer* lost its parlor car in 1937, the *Mount Royal* its sleeping car in 1947.

A disastrous strike on the Rutland Railroad ended all passenger service on the Rutland in June 1953. From then on, the B&M name trains terminated at Bellows Falls, with connecting trains on the Connecticut River line carrying passengers to White River Junction. For several decades the B&M operated a lucrative milk train business over the Cheshire, these trains connecting with shipments into Bellows Falls from the Rutland Railroad.

President of the Boston & Maine from 1931 through 1951 was Edward S. French, who began his long and distinguished career on the railroad while still in college as a clerk, ticket agent, and messenger. He was known for his personal involvement with daily activity on the system and well liked and respected by the railroad's employees. His home was in Chester, Vermont, and the *Cheshire* schedule was arranged to make it convenient for him to "commute" from Bellows Falls to Boston, a two-hour, 25 minute ride on this commodious streamline train (Unit 6000) with buffet service. From Bellows Falls he would go by car the last 13 miles to Chester, while the *Cheshire* continued on to White River Junction.

It was on its morning, inbound run on January 19, 1945 that the *Cheshire* had an unfortunate accident when it derailed and crashed into the Walpole, New Hampshire freight house. Fortunately, there were no serious injuries, but Unit 6000 was damaged badly in front. Probably a lot of food and coffee went flying in the buffet, too. One does not know if President French was aboard.

By the time of the April 27, 1952 timetable change, President French had retired and the *Cheshire* began terminating at Bellows Falls, though there was still a connection to White River Junction. (At the same time, Unit 6000 began service between Boston and Troy, New York as the *Minuteman*. It returned briefly to *Cheshire* service in early December, 1956. It was retired in April and donated to the Edaville Railroad)

The B&M acquired its first three Budd RDCs early in 1952, and these were such a resounding success that three more were ordered the following year. The Cheshire Branch was assigned one of the cars, and the timetable of September 27, 1953 shows train No. 5505 as a Budd "Highliner," leaving Boston at 12:30 p.m. for a round trip to White River Junction via Bellows Falls, returning the following morning at 10:25 a.m.

After 1954 the names *Green Mountain* and *Mount Royal* disappeared from the timetable, though the trains continued, and the *Cheshire* kept its name until the end. In late 1956 the B&M experimented with joining a train to Bellows Falls (No. 5503) and Troy (the *Minuteman*) as far as Fitchburg. As explained in the chapter on the Gloucester Branch, midway in the trip two Budd RDCs would be sent their separate ways with one operator in each cab. The following year the practice was extended to a second train, half of which was the *Cheshire*, the other half (No. 59) going to Williamstown.

Passenger service on the Cheshire Branch came to an

end on May 18, 1958, its trains now terminating at Fitchburg. Service was actually to have ended May 10 but it was prolonged one week as a result of legal action by the State of New Hampshire. That was the best they could do; Mr. McGinnis prevailed.

The colorful American entrepreneur, F. Nelson Blount, established a tourist railroad—the Monadnock, Steamtown, & Northern—at Keene in 1961 (after several weeks on the Claremont & Concord). Later he moved the operation to North Walpole and used some 13 miles of track east to Westmoreland. He brought most of the rolling stock from Pleasure Island, an amusement park in Wakefield, Massachusetts, where he had been collecting it. His vision was to build a standard gauge rail museum at Keene, but negotiations with the Boston & Maine and the State of New Hampshire were not successful, so he

shortly moved the whole operation across the Connecticut River and conducted his operations on former Rutland trackage with more satisfaction. A ride on Blount's wonderful Cheshire Branch MS&N is described in the Epilogue.

The B&M continued to use the Branch for occasional freight service (oversize cars which wouldn't clear the Bellows Falls tunnel on the Connecticut River line were frequent visitors), but the business was never great enough to justify the heavy costs of maintaining the trackage. The Cheshire Branch was finally abandoned north of Winchendon in 1972, having been out of service some four years.

Pacific 3628 is making quite a show of its passage through Westmoreland, New Hampshire on January 9, 1951. Stephen R. Payne photo.

Top: *Stephen R. Payne became famous for a sign he would place near the track, ahead of where he was shooting. Engineers were requested to "Please make smoke—photographer ahead." Pacific 3628 is returning to Boston after its westbound run shown on the previous page.*
Below: *Extra 1706 west at Fitzwilliam, New Hampshire with a high-and-wide load on this clear-as-a-bell day, September 17, 1966. Donald S. Robinson photo.*

Above: The white flags are flapping in the wind as Consolidation 2730 highballs past the semaphores with an extra freight at Winchendon, Massachusetts on December 30, 1950. Stephen R. Payne photo.

Below: We're at Cold River, New Hampshire on January 4, 1969 as Extra 4265 east is moving toward Boston late this afternoon. Donald S. Robinson captured one of the few Fs still operating.

THE PETERBORO BRANCH

The year 1874 saw the opening of rail service from Worcester to Peterboro, a distance of 52 miles. The first 36 miles to Winchendon at the intersection of the Cheshire Railroad comprised the Boston, Barre & Gardner Railroad, while the next 16 miles to Peterboro were the Monadnock Railroad, leased by the BB&G. The Cheshire Railroad took over the operation of both of these in 1880; it in turn came under the control of the Fitchburg in 1890. Finally, in 1900, the B&M leased the Fitchburg.

Additional operation north of Peterboro was provided by the Peterboro and Hillsboro for 18 miles, and from Hillsboro to Contoocook by the Contoocook Valley Railroad. After the great September hurricane of 1936, the B&M severed the line at Peterboro. Even before this, however, passenger trains had not operated all the way from Worcester to Contoocook for some time. In 1933, for example, two daily round trips ran between Worcester and Peterboro, one between Peterboro and Contoocook, and one between Winchendon and Contoocook.

By 1943 only a single Worcester-Peterboro daily round trip remained, and it survived only into 1952 when the economics of up-country passenger railroading made its operation prohibitive. The B&M arranged that this train, No. 8111 outbound and No. 8118 inbound, would connect daily at Winchendon with a Cheshire Branch train (outbound, the *Green Mountain Flyer* daily; inbound, the *Green Mountain Flyer* on Sunday and train No. 5508 weekdays) to provide additional flexibility for riders. The arrival of the two trains at Winchendon could be quite colorful, especially during the last days when the B&M leased a New Haven RS3 (No. 561 was one) in the warm orange and forest green scheme to head the Peterboro train. The Sunday train was discontinued in the fall of 1949.

In the early forties a local freight worked the line between Gardner and Peterboro. In 1954 this local was listed as working Monday through Friday; in 1962 it worked Monday-Wednesday-Friday and handled duties on both this and the Cheshire Branch also as far as Troy, so it is clear that patronage was down considerably by then.

Left: David C. Bartlett made this charming portrait of the southbound local in April 1949. Mogul 1427 is on the point. **Above**: Scenically, the Peterboro line was among the B&M's most special. Here the road's first RS-2, No. 1500, in the distinguished black and red scheme, pulls a southbound local freight on October 8, 1952. Collection of Bob's photos. **Below**: Ten years later, Russell Munroe caught the same locomotive at East Jaffrey, New Hampshire, late in the afternoon on the day before Christmas.

Above: The Peterboro local is loading mail and express in April 1949. Winchendon was served both by the Peterboro and Cheshire Branches, with trackage shared by them for a short distance here. **Below**: Another shared depot was Gardner, Massachusetts, at the junction of the Peterboro Branch with the Fitchburg Division mainline. The Peterboro train is headed for Worcester. Two photos, David C. Bartlett.

Above: The Peterboro local disappears from Indian Hill into what *Trains* magazine publisher A. C. Kalmbach once described as "wonderously green New England scenery." Stanley W. Cook photo.

Below: The engineer of Mogul 1470 is looking back over his train prior to departing Jefferson station in September 1949. David C. Bartlett photo.

Above: Mogul 1366 makes a dramatic sweep past U. S. Route 202 at Peterboro on January 8, 1951.
Below: Noone Street, Peterboro is the sight of this little one-car freight on December 1, 1949.

Right: This unusual view at the Peterboro Depot would soon be impossible, as a corrugated structure was later built on the spot where the photographer is standing.

Below: The crew turns Mogul 1404 on the Armstrong turntable for the run south. Four photos, Stephen R. Payne.

VII

ON THE RIVER'S SPINE
The Connecticut River Valley

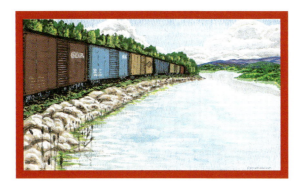

I have had a most delightful excursion along the enchanting Valley of the Connecticut—of which I dare not speak at present—for it is just now the topic which I am a little mad upon. It is a perfect stream for a poet. In short I recommend you, if you have the power, make the tour that I have done, and you will have made one of the most beautiful, for natural scenery, in the world.

Washington Irving
Letter of August 1, 1832

Like the other lines of the Boston & Maine, the Connecticut River Line was assembled from a number of much smaller railroads. The southernmost of these, the Connecticut River Railroad, was built from Springfield to South Deerfield, Massachusetts, in 1846, being extended to the Vermont line shortly after to meet the Vermont & Massachusetts Railroad which went as far as Brattleboro, Vermont. (From this same point on the Vermont line, the CRR leased the Ashuelot Railroad to Keene, described in the next section.) In 1877 the CRR acquired the Vermont Valley Railroad to make the next step north as far as Bellows Falls (which the VVR reached in 1851). Next came the Sullivan County Railroad which went as far as Windsor (built in the 1840s), and finally there was the Connecticut &

Passumpsic Rivers Railroad north of White River Junction (opened as far as St. Johnsbury by 1850), its ownership passing briefly to the Connecticut River Railroad in 1885, to the Boston & Lowell in 1887, and later that year to the Boston & Maine. The balance of the Connecticut River Railroad's properties came into B&M control in 1893.

The 14 miles of track between Windsor and White River Junction never became part of the B&M; this remained the property of its builder, the Central Vermont. Indeed, because of a stiff rivalry between these two roads, some eight miles of parallel trackage was built between Dole Junction and Brattleboro before a truce was called. For a time it appeared that redundant, unnecessary tracks might be built far up the Valley, from Cornish, across the river from Windsor, to Lebanon.

The Connecticut River Line figured prominently in the B&M's passenger business. We have already had a look at the Boston-Montreal service north of White River Junction, and later, in the White Mountains section, we will touch on the varnish to that area. Plying the central core of the Connecticut River Line between Spingfield and White River Junction were no fewer than six trains. In the daytime, one could ride in style north from Springfield at 9:30 a.m., 12:32 p.m. on the *Day White Mountains*, and at 4:00 p.m. Nighttime trains were the 8:40 p.m. *Connecticut Yankee*, the 12:40 a.m. *Montrealer*, and the 4:55 a.m. *Overnighter*.

This freight from Mechanicville, New York has detoured over the Delaware & Hudson via Whitehall, New York, and Rutland, Vermont, where it joined the Green Mountain Railroad. Here it joins the Connecticut River *Line at Bellows Falls, Vermont, on February 26, 1967 behind GP-9 1721. Conductor John J. Falvey is standing on the front of the locomotive. Russell F. Munroe photo.*

CONNECTICUT RIVER LOCAL FREIGHTS

1942
[frequency not known]

E. Deerfield-Turners Falls-Keene*
Keene-East Deerfield*

Northampton-E. Deerfield-
Holyoke-Easthampton

Bellows Falls-Windsor

1954
[daily frequency in ( )]

E. Deerfield-Keene (6)

E. Deerfield-Turners Falls-
Northampton (6)

Northampton-Easthampton-
Holyoke & return (6)

Bellows Falls-Claremont-Windsor (6)

E. Deerfield-Springfield (6)

1962
[daily frequency in ( )]

E. Deerfield-Keene (6)

E. Deerfield-Turners Falls-
Easthampton (3)

E. Deerfield-White River Jct. (3)*
White River Jct-E. Deerfield (3)*

*Indicates a train requiring two days for a round trip

CONNECTICUT RIVER MAINLINE FREIGHTS

	1942	1954	1962
Springfield-Wells River	1**	1	1
Springfield-White River Junction	2	2	1
White River Junction-Berlin	1	1	1
White River Junction-Wells River (and onto the Canadian Pacific)	2	2	2
East Deerfield-White River Junction	1	0	0
Springfield-Mechanicville	1	1	1

**Each unit represents a round trip.

The level of mainline service seems to
have remained amazingly consistent.

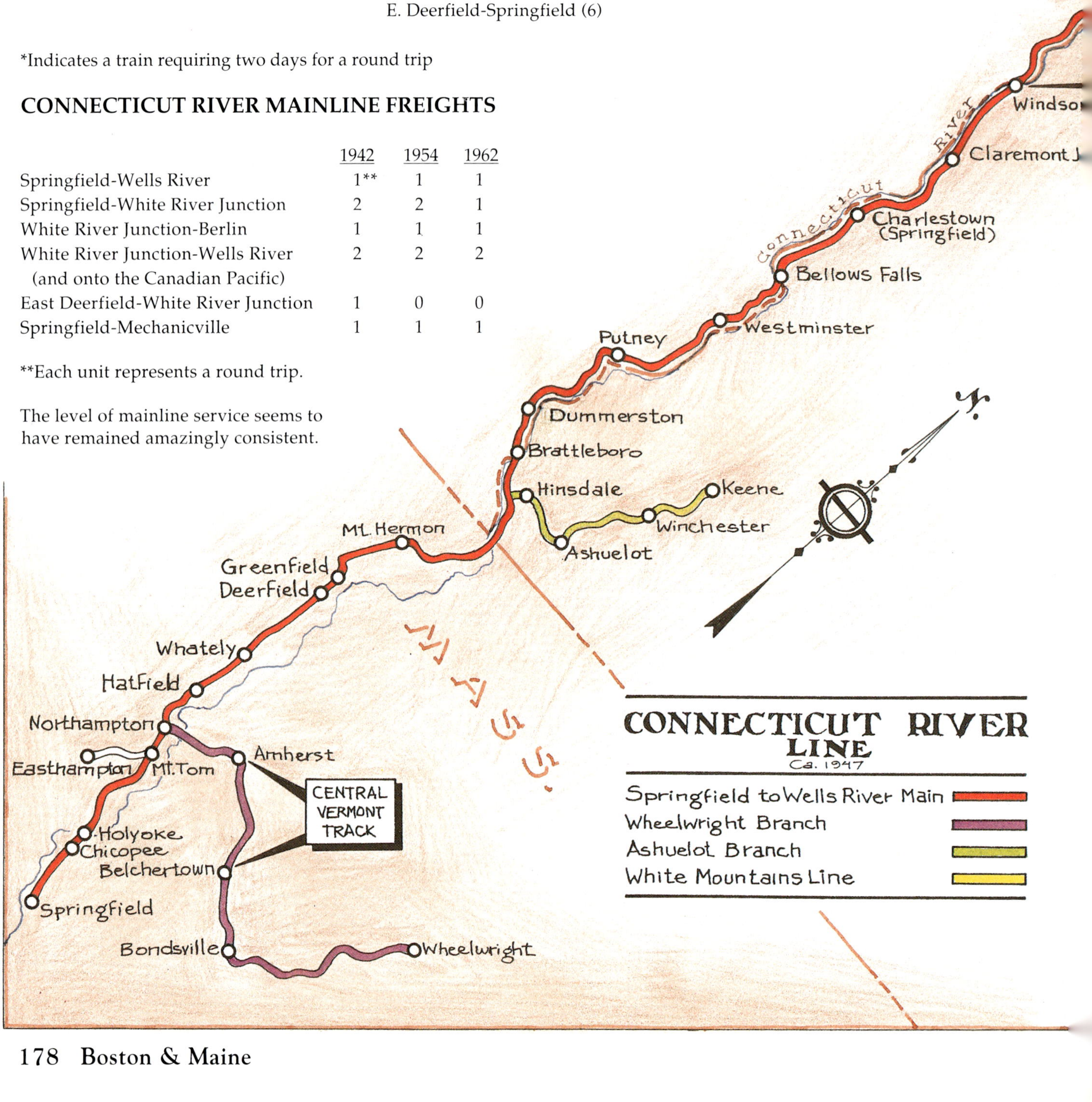

CONNECTICUT RIVER LINE
Ca. 1947

Springfield to Wells River Main ▬
Wheelwright Branch ▬
Ashuelot Branch ▬
White Mountains Line ▬

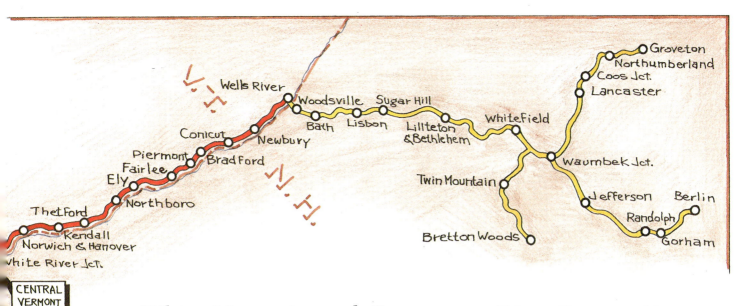

White Mountains and Connecticut River Points 69
To Springfield-New Haven-New York-Philadelphia-Baltimore and Washington

CENTRAL VERMONT TRACK

a Stops to receive passengers for north of Springfield.

b Motor Coach from and to Whitefield.

c By connecting train.

d Stops to receive passengers for south of White River Jct.

e Stops to discharge passengers.

f Stops on signal to discharge or receive passengers.

g Coach passengers change on arrival at New Haven and Springfield.

h Sun. lv. Springfield 8 15 p.m., ar. Hartford 8 57 p.m., New Haven 9 50 p.m., Bridgeport 10 19 p.m., Stamford 10 51 p.m., New York 11 40 p.m.

n Stops to discharge passengers from north of Springfield.

r Sundays leave New Haven 8 35 p.m. arrive New York (Penn. Sta.) 10 01 p.m.

s Coach train. Sleeping car train leave New Haven 2 20 a.m., arrive Phila. (30th St.) 5 43 a.m., arrive Baltimore 7 25 a.m., arrive Washington 8 15 a.m.

t Stops to receive passengers for Greenfield and beyond.

u No checked baggage handled on this train.

v Stops to receive passengers.

x Stops to receive passengers for St. Albans and beyond.

y Flag stop until Sept. 7, inc.

• Daily.

£ Stops to discharge passengers from south of White River Jct. or to receive passengers for north of Woodsville.

‡ Stops to discharge passengers until Sept. 7, inc.

△ Outbound trains stop only to receive passengers and inbound trains stop only to discharge passengers at N.Y. 125th St.

GCT Grand Central Terminal.

❀ "The Cheshire" limited equipment. All reserved seats. All coach class tickets (except restricted excursion and furlough tickets) will be accepted. Buffet service.

● No checked baggage handled on the North Wind except only to or from Bretton Woods-Fabyan.

Southbound			Washingtonian	78	Cheshire ❀				Day White Mts. Exp.	Connecticut Yankee	No. Wind ●	Valley Exp.	4308	6056	Night White Mts Exp
			Daily	Daily	exSun				72 exSun	74 Daily	70 exSat	7062u Sun	exSun	Sun	76 Sun
			A M	A M	A M				A M	P M	P M	P M	P M	P M	P M
Groveton.........B&M.R.R., N. H.	Lv		...	...	...	...	...	...	b7 00	...	runs	b1 20	...	...	Sun only
Lancaster	"		...	...	...	...	...	...	b7 35	...	until	b1 55	2 55	...	until
Whitefield.........	"	Ar	...	...	...	...	...	...	b8 00	...	Sept.	b2 20	3 30	...	August
Berlin...............	"	Lv	...	...	...	...	...	...	7 10	...	15	1 25	...	...	25, inc.
Gorham............	"		...	...	...	...	...	...	7 20	...	inc.	1 36	...	...	also
Jefferson.............	"		...	...	...	...	...	...	7 52	...	...	2 12	...	...	Mon.
Whitefield	"	Ar	...	...	...	...	...	...	8 08	...	...	2 28	...	...	Sept. 2
B. WOODS-FABYAN	"	Lv	...	...	...	...	...	...	...	...	12 20	...	...	...	8 30
WHITEFIELD...B&M.R.R.	"	Lv	...	...	...	...	...	...	8 15	...	12 50	...	2 35	3 30	9 05
Littleton & Bethlehem	"		...	...	...	...	...	...	8 40	...	1 10	...	3 01	3 52	9 32
Sugar Hill...........	"		...	...	...	...	...	...	8 55	...	1 25	...	3 14	f4 05	9 48
Lisbon................	"		...	...	...	...	...	...	9 00	...	...	...	3 20	4 10	......
Bath	"		...	...	...	...	...	...	9 10	...	...	...	3 30	v4 20	......
WOODSVILLE....	"	Ar	...	...	...	...	...	...	9 20	...	1 45	...	3 40	4 30	10 13
WOODSVILLE....	"	Lv	...	...	stream	...	...	...	9 30	...	1 50	runs	3 55	4 40	10 20
WELLS RIVER .	Vt.		...	1 20	line	...	...	...	...	...	...	Sun.	...	...	......
Newbury..............	"		...	...	train	...	...	...	d9 40	...	...	only	4 05	f4 50	......
Conicut	"		...	...	to	...	...	...	y9 45	...	v2 04	until	4 10	...	10 35
Bradford...........	"		...	y1 37	Boston	...	...	...	9 53	...	...	Aug.	4 18	5 02	......
Piermont............	"		...	...	all	...	...	...	...	...	...	25	4 24	...	......
Fairlee (Lake Morey)	"		...	...	seats	...	...	...	10 05	...	2 20	inc.	4 40	5 15	10 53
Ely (Fairlee Lake)	"		...	...	reserved	...	...	...	f10 11	...	...	Mon.	4 46	...	......
Northboro............	"		...	...	❀	...	...	...	f10 15	...	...	Sept.	4 51	f5 26	......
Thetford............	"		...	...	...	...	...	...	10 21	...	...	2 and	4 56	e5 31	......
Kendall.............	"		...	...	...	...	...	...	f10 29	...	...	Sun.	v5 04	...	......
Norwich, Vt. & Hanover ..	N. H.		...	...	...	...	...	...	10 39	...	...	Sept.	5 14	5 49	......
Wilder...............	"		...	...	...	...	...	...	...	...	...	8 & 15	5 18	...	......
WHITE RIVER JCT. ..	Vt.	Ar	...	2 20	...	...	...	...	10 50	...	3 05	...	5 25	6 00	11 35

Boston and Maine R.R.			732 Daily	7052 Sun	78 exSun	5506u exSun	712 exSun	702 Sun	72 exSun	74 Daily	70 exSat	7062u Sun	728 exSun	7060 Sun	76 Mon.
			A M	A M	A M	A M	A M	A M	A M	P M	P M	P M	A M	A M	A M
WHITE RIVER JCT.CV.Ry.	Vt.	Lv	1 45	2 45	2 45	6 05	7 20	11 15	11 15	1 53	3 20	5 35	5 45	6 45	12 20
Windsor . . . .B&M.R.R.	"		...	3 08	3 08	6 27	7 45	11 38	11 41	2 25	...	5 57	6 18	7 10	...
Claremont Jct.......	N. H.	Lv	...	3 35	3 35	6 37	8 00	11 50	11 55	2 37	3 56	6 09	6 35	7 23	...
North Charlestown	"		...	...	...	...	8 08	...	...	...	...	...	...	...	...
CHARLESTOWN	"	{ Ar	...	e3 49	f3 49	6 50	8 18	12 03	12 09	2 49	...	...	6 48	7 38	...
	"	{ Lv	...	e3 49	f3 49	6 50	8 18	12 03	12 13	2 49	...	...	6 53	7 38	...
South Charlestown	"		...	...	...	...	f8 24	...	...	...	...	...	...	...	...
BELLOWS FALLS	Vt.	Ar	2 42	4 01	4 01	7 05	8 31	12 16	12 24	3 00	4 23	6 34	7 05	7 48	...
BELLOWS FALLS	"	Lv	2 42	4 13	4 13	...	8 35	12 16	12 30	3 05	4 23	6 34	7 25	7 53	...
Westminster	"		...	...	...	...	8 43	...	...	...	...	...	...	...	...
East Putney...........	"		...	...	...	...	...	...	...	...	...	...	...	...	...
Putney	"		...	...	...	...	9 01	...	12 52	r3 24	...	...	f7 45	...	...
Dummerston.........	"		...	...	...	...	f9 07	...	...	...	...	...	...	...	...
Brattleboro	"		3 20	4 52	4 52	...	9 23	12 54	1 10	3 42	5 03	7 11	8 05	8 32	...
EAST NORTHFIELD ..	Mass.		...	f5 09	f5 09	...	9 50	1 09	1 28	3 57	...	7 26	8 25	8 47	...
Mt. Hermon.........	"		...	...	...	...	9 58	...	...	...	...	...	...	...	...
Bernardston.........	"		...	...	...	...	10 06	...	...	...	...	...	...	...	...
GREENFIELD	"	Ar	...	5 30	5 30	...	10 17	1 30	1 48	4 17	...	7 45	8 45	9 04	...
GREENFIELD	"	Lv	...	5 45	5 42	...	10 35	1 30	2 05	4 22	...	7 45	9 05	9 10	...
Northampton ...	"		...	6 12	6 20	...	11 03	1 54	2 33	4 50	...	8 08	9 35	9 40	...
Holyoke ...	"		...	6 29	6 38	...	11 17	2 07	2 50	5 05	...	8 20	9 53	9 55	...
SPRINGFIELD .	"	Ar	4 48	6 48	7 02	...	11 35	2 25	3 12	5 23	...	...	10 15	10 15	...

N. Y., N. H. & H. R.R.			169	91	405		51	79	85	59	97	61	417	99	101	167
SPRINGFIELD....N.H.RR.	"	Lv	4 59	7 37	7 45	...	11 55	2 40	3 32	5 45	h8 00	...	10 45	11 00	...
Hartford	Conn.	Ar	5 31	8 15	8 17	...	12 27	3 12	4 08	6 13	h8 40	n7 07	n9 17	11 20	11 34	...
NEW HAVEN.......	"	{ Ar	6 23	9 08	9 00	...	1 25	3 55	5 07	7 20	h10 00	n7 50	10 00	1 10	12 40	n5 10
	"	{ Lv	6 33	9 15	9 00	...	1 30	4 00	5 17	7 25	h10 10	n7 55	10 10	1 35	12 50	n5 20
Bridgeport	"	Ar	6 55	9 35	c9 34	...	1 50	4 19	5 37	7 46	h10 30	...	10 30	1 55	1 10	...
Stamford	"		...	10 07	c10 05	...	2 22	4 48	6 07	8 16	h10 57	...	10 57	2 54	1 52	...
NEW YORK { 125th St.	N. Y. △		...	10 44	10 25	...	3 00	5 25	6 44	8 54	h11 35	...	11 35	3 48	2 43	...
{ GCTerm.	"	Ar	...	10 55	10 35	...	3 10	5 35	6 55	9 05	h11 45	9 20	11 45	4 00	2 55	7 00
New Haven, Ct. (coach passengers to Penn. R.R. change here)		Lv	...	...	...	...	2 28	...	5 12	r8 23	s1 15	...	...		Daily	
New York(Penn. Sta.)		Ar	8 10	...	...	...	2 45	...	6 45	r10 00	s2 48	...	...	1 15	2 20	6 33
No. Philadelphia Penn. R.R.	Pa.		10 11	...	...	...	6 01	...	8 24	11 58	s4 54	...	...	4 54	3 53	8 10
Philadelphia (30th St.) ..	"		10 20	...	...	...	6 11	...	8 34	12 07	s5 03	...	...	5 03	5 43	10 11
Baltimore (Penn. Sta.) ..	Md.		12 22	...	...	...	7 42	...	10 04	...	s7 05	...	...	7 05	7 25	12 22
WASHINGTON ..	D.C.	Ar	1 15	...	...	...	8 25	...	10 45	...	s8 00	...	...	8 00	8 15	1 15
			P M	A M	A M		P M	P M	P M	P M	A M	P M	P M	A M	A M	P M

Above left: *Train 720 is at Northampton, Massachusetts behind Pacific 3620 this crystalline winter day in 1946. Donald S. Robinson photo.*

Center left: *Central Vermont Extra 707 South is on the B&M at Charlestown, New Hampshire on June 26, 1950, making much soot. Donald G. Hills photo.*

Below left: *The ubiquitous "Sacred Cow," today the Springfield-Greenfield local, arrives at Deerfield at 2:53 p.m. on October 13, 1956. The passengers waiting here will be able to connect conveniently at Greenfield with a Boston train. Stanley W. Cook photo.*

Above right: *The conductor is climbing down in the distance as FT 4210 with its northbound freight pauses at Brattleboro. Arthur E. Mitchell photo.*

Below right: *Central Vermont 4-6-2 231 heads train 72, the southbound Day White Mountains, at Greenfield in 1950. Train 57, a 39-stops local train from Boston to Troy, New York, is on the left, and to its left can be seen a Maine Central E-7, heading up a Boston-bound Minuteman, its headlight reflecting off the shiny local passenger train. Russell F. Munroe photo.*

Opposite, top left: *F-2 4226 A&B is pulling into Bellows Falls with a northbound passenger train in the early fifties. At right is the large Boston & Maine/Rutland freight house. Arthur E. Mitchell photo.*

Opposite, center: *Link Belt crane W-330 has the sad task of cutting down the ball signal at Bellows Falls on May 2, 1968. Russell F. Munroe photo.*

Left: *Southbound train 76, the Ambassador, has left White River Junction and is seen here at the lower end of the yard passing a B&M freight behind an RS-3 and Switcher 1269 with a long string of cars, July 16, 1966. George F. Melvin photo/J. Emmons Lancaster collection.*

Above: *On the morning June 26, 1950, B&M train 712 is carrying through coaches from White River Junction over the Claremont, New Hampshire "High Bridge" on their way to Grand Central Terminal in New York City. Locomotive power today is Central Vermont 4-8-2 No. 601. The fourth and sixth cars are "American Flyer" cars from the B&M and New Haven, respectively. The 1930 bridge was constructed with piers to carry two tracks, but girders for only one track were ever installed. One stone pier from old bridge is visible just right of center. Donald G. Hills photo.*

Left: *One does not often see photographs of Windsor, Vermont, especially color ones of steam in 1947. Windsor marked one end of B&M trackage which, for the 14 miles to White River Junction, was owned by the Central Vermont, and shared under a trackage rights agreement.*

Below left: *A work train—Extra 1231 North—is in the midst of lush, rain softened greenery at Newbury, Vermont this June 24, 1969. Two photos, Donald S. Robinson.*

Above: Behind Central Vermont 4-8-2 No. 603, the northbound Ambassador is into CV territory just moments after leaving White River Junction on April 30, 1950.

Right: Central Vermont train 332, the Ambassador, crosses the White River at Hartford, Vermont on June 26, 1950. Two photos, Donald G. Hills.

Three action shots at Wells River, Vermont.
Top left: *Train 32 from Montreal waits for train 372 from Berlin, New Hampshire to couple up for the run to White River Junction in August 1959. Budd RDC 6205 will lead the train south. Donald G. Hills photo.*

Center left: *RS-3 1541 is in charge of a milk train for Boston.*

Left: *And here's a rarity—the departing Barre & Chelsea local heads west. That RPO-coach combine has six-wheel trucks, no less. Two photos, Arthur E. Mitchell.*

Above: *George Melvin chose September 5, 1966 to photograph this southbound freight at Barnet, Vermont behind GP-7s 1555 and 1569. We're on the Canadian Pacific at this point and the train is 803. J. Emmons Lancaster collection.*

Left: *A southbound Canadian Pacific reefer train for Springfield is a just a few yards from B&M territory as it rounds the bend into the Wells River depot. Arthur E. Mitchell photo.*

THE WHEELWRIGHT BRANCH

The Wheelwright Branch is the 38 mile western-most section of the former Central Mass Branch (page 156) which was broken in two on September 21, 1938 by the great New England Hurricane. Truth to tell, the B&M had actually embargoed the middle of the line the prior June anyway, and freight service in recent years had been accomplished by two locals working toward Rutland from Boston and Northampton, respectively.

The Depression had already taken a heavy toll on the Central Mass. In a dramatic cost-cutting measure, the B&M secured trackage rights in the summer of 1931 over the Central Vermont's parallel mainline from Norwottuck south some ten miles to Canal Junction, and in the summer of 1932 over 15 miles of the Boston & Albany's parallel Ware River Branch from Forest Lake to Barre Junction. The remaining trackage represented a scant 20 miles of the original Central Mass. The last through passenger train arrived in Northampton from Boston in April 1932.

Following this, freight service was provided by a daily-except-Sunday local to Wheelwright, where a paper mill provided significant business until it closed in 1973. The Diamond National Mill at Bondsville was also an active customer. In April 1974 service was down to a once a week extra. Maintenance was almost non-existant, the track conditions so bad that the local eventually required two days for the out and back schedule on a 10 mph limit.

Left: The brakeman has thrown our switch for Extra 1117 West at Canal Junction, Massachusetts on March 8, 1969, to bring the train onto Central Vermont trackage. Donald S. Robinson photo.

Above: The power for third class train 7701 pauses at Bondsville Depot on March 31, 1971. The station was still an active agency then, with a functioning order board, but it was closed on September 28, 1973. This trackage—the west end of the Central Mass—was abandoned in the late seventies. H. Bentley Crouch photo.

Below: Train H2 behind Mogul 1421 is steaming it up aplenty at a grade crossing with a pretty good revenue load at Northampton, Massachusetts in the winter of 1946. Donald S. Robinson photo.

THE ASHUELOT BRANCH

With the building of the Cheshire Railroad to Keene in 1848 (page 166), the Connecticut River Railroad quickly envisioned the profitable opportunities to be explored should a connection be made from their trackage on the River to Keene. Nature, in her wisdom, had already provided a level right of way by the Ashuelot River, and so, in 1850, 22 miles of new track were laid along this route between South Vernon—near the point where the Ashuelot River flows into the Connecticut—and Keene. Appropriately enough, this was called the Ashuelot Railroad.

The road was leased at first by the Connecticut River Railroad, the Cheshire Railroad assuming the lease from 1860 until 1877, when it again was taken up by the Connecticut for another 16 years. In 1893 the Boston & Maine took control of the Connecticut River Railroad, and the Ashuelot line along with it.

Passenger service on this scenic line dwindled in the same pattern as the rest of the B&M system. Where in 1900 there were six round trips a day, just after World War II there were but two. Sunday service ended after the summer of 1949, and in 1952 a morning mixed train was all that was left of passenger service. Previously

the morning run from East Northfield had consumed some 50 minutes in traversing the branch to Keene. The mixed train stretched this to two hours, and even this was from Dole Junction so that passengers couldn't connect with the mainline at East Northfield. Amazingly, this little morning accommodation train was still listed in the June 1958 timetable, a significant fact considering how deep the passenger cuts had been already.

Of course, it wasn't the passenger revenue keeping the train alive, it was the movement of merchandise that did so. And considering the age of the coach which probably brought up the rear, one supposes that there wasn't much extra expense involved. Wartime business in 1942 included two daily trains between East Deerfield and Keene, running in opposite directions, though by 1954 a single, daily round-trip was able to handle the activity by itself. Beginning in 1961, this same train was sufficiently idle that it could continue on to Bellows Falls to handle work there as well. Businesses along the line included the Hinsdale Paper mill, Ashuelot paper, a leather company in Winchester, the Cheshire Farmer's Exchange, and the Weeterau food warehouse.

Miles	Rail-road	Sun A M	exSun A M	exSun A M	Sun P M	READ DOWN		READ UP	Sun A M	exSun P M	exSun P M	Sun P M
0.0	N. H.	11 30	11 30	3 45	11 10	Lv New York G.C.T.	N. Y.	Ar	....	3 10	9 05	9 05
55.6	..	12 41	12 41	5 25	12 44	...Bridgeport	Conn.	...	...	1 50	7 46	7 46
72.3	..	1 05	1 05	t5 55	1 20	......New Haven.. ...	..			1 25	7 20	7 20
108.9	..	2 08	2 08	7 00	2 47	...Hartford	..	Ar	12 27	6 17	6 17	
134.3	..	2 43	2 43	t7 42	3 23	Ar Springfield...........	Mass.	Lv	11 55	5 45	5 45	
		7055	717	73	7051				712	74	74	
0.0	B&M	3 00	3 00	8 30	3 55	Lv Springfield..........	Mass.	Ar	11 30	5 23	5 23	
49.7	..	4 34	4 39	10 37	5 07	Ar East Northfield ..	..	Lv	9 50	3 57	3 57	
	..	7353	7305	7301	7351				7350	7300	7302	7302
49.7	..	4 37	4 52	10 49	8 45	Lv E. NORTHFIELD	..	Ar	8 34	9 34	3 44	3 44
51.9	..	f4 42	f4 58	f10 54	f8 50	...Dole Jct.	N. H.	...	8 29	9 29	3 39	3 39
54.5	..	f4 48	5 04	11 00	f8 56	......Hinsdale........	..	....	8 20	9 20	3 30	f3 30
58.0	..	f4 56	5 12	11 08	f9 04	....Ashuelot...	..	...	f8 12	9 12	3 22	f3 22
60.2	..	f5 02	5 18	11 14	f9 10	....Winchester.......	..	...	8 07	9 07	3 16	f3 16
65.6	..	f5 12	f5 28	f11 25	f9 20	...Westport	..	...	f7 57	f8 57	f3 05	f3 05
68.2	..	f5 18	5 34	11 31	f9 26	....West Swanzey.......	..	....	f7 52	8 52	2 59	f2 59
70.4	..	...	...	f11 36	f9 31	...Swanzey	..	...			2 53	f2 53
73.7	..	5 30	5 46	11 45	9 40	Ar KEENE.............	..	Lv	7 40	8 40	2 45	2 45
		P M	P M	A M	A M				A M	A M	P M	P M

4-25-48 XL

Considering how remote were the towns along the Ashuelot Branch, twice a day passenger service seems quite adequate. Table 81 is excerpted from the April 25, 1948 Northern New England Travel Guide published by the Boston & Maine. Author's collection.

Left: *Passenger service on the Ashuelot Branch was frequently handled by a gas-electric car, such as unit 1195 seen here at Hinsdale, New Hampshire in 1946.* **Below**: *From the rear platform of the same car, we have a fine view of the local freight on the passing track at Hinsdale. Two photos, Donald S. Robinson.*

RAILS TO THE WHITE MOUNTAINS

Younger generations, however interested, will find it hard to visualize scenes of rolling wheels on many Pullmans, panting steam power, and the hectic activity which accompanied the enormous amount of resort traffic in the White Mountains. Historians of a new day may with diligence still seek out traces of abandoned roadbeds, old bridge abutments and the like, but evidence of the equipment and the men who spent so much effort in maintaining and operating this vast network becomes increasingly harder to find with the passing of time. Fortunate are we who saw it first hand!

H. Arnold Wilder
"Passengers to the White Mountains"
B&M Bulletin

Reaching northeast another hundred miles from Wells River, far into the north woods, are the lines to Berlin and Groteton, New Hampshire.

The White Mountains Railroad, building east from Woodsville, reached Littleton in 1853. It was the first railroad into the White Mountains and quickly benefitted from a growing tourist business. The Boston, Concord & Montreal Railroad leased the White Mountains line in 1859, spearheading further construction to Lancaster in 1870, Groton in 1872, and in 1874 from Wing Road to Fabyan. In the meantime, the completion of the Mount Washington Cog Railway in 1869 helped bring thousands more summertime visitors for decades thereafter. This pristine landscape of woods and mountains was home to a multitude of summer hotels for affluent tourists from the city.

As we have seen on virtually every other B&M line, and in truth throughout the U.S., the level of service after World War II declined. The loss of patronage was at first slight, but with the advent of the 1950s the slide of business became precipitous. And thus it was with the wonderful trains to the White Mountains as well.

In 1946 one could still enjoy Friday night sleeper service to Bretton Woods-Fabyan on the Night White Mountains Express. With the post-war optimism which was so contagious, the B&M and the New Haven created the *North Wind*, a new coach-parlor car train designed for fast daily-except-Sunday service between New York City and resort stops all the way to Fabyan.

The *Mountaineer*, covered by Unit 6000 during the summers from 1942 to 1952, was another very popular train which capitalized on the region's breathtaking landscapes. The train arrived in the White Mountains

via the scenic Conway Branch and Maine Central line through Crawford Notch.

But better highways were abuilding and Americans were affording more and more automobiles. In 1950 the *Mountaineer* was reduced to a Friday, Saturday, and Sunday operation, lasting only through 1956. The *Night White Mountains* continued its weekend service faithfully through 1955, but the *North Wind* was trimmed to three days a week in 1950, then was dropped until 1955. It ran daily in 1955 and 1956 then sadly disappeared forever.

The final chapter in north country passenger service was written in 1961, when, at summer's dusk, a single Budd RDC left Berlin for the last time.

Happily, rail service continued to the area with a reasonably lucrative freight operation. The B&M handled considerable freight to and from the paper mills in Berlin well into the 1960s, operating daily except Sunday freights between White River Junction and Berlin. Working part of this same trackage was a Woodsville-Groton local freight on a two day up-and-back schedule. By the sixties, this local freight was working six days between Groton and Littleton only, reflecting something of a downturn in business and lack of maintenance. It is now operated as the New Hampshire & Vermont Railroad in connection with the Lamoille Valley Railroad.

The majesty of the White Mountains was captured brilliantly by Richard Story at Randolph, New Hampshire on March 31, 1978. The train is southbound UJ-2, the Berlin-White River Junction freight.

Right: The relatively dense industry of Berlin, New Hampshire is well illustrated in this Herman Shaner photo from July 1969. J. Emmons Lancaster collection.

Below right: GP-9 1728 leads UJ-2 across the Maine Central diamond at Waumbeck Junction at 6:30 p.m., June 26, 1967. At this time, just two ball signals remained on the B&M: this one and the one at Whitefield. H. Bentley Crouch photo.

Far right, top: Train UJ-4 is behind GP-7 1560 on June 3, 1969. The scene is the Androscoggin River at Gorham, New Hampshire. Immediately behind the diesels are two hoppers, custom modified to handle wood chips. Donald S. Robinson photo.

Far right, bottom: Russell F. Munroe made this early evening photograph of F-7 4266 pulling freight across the trestle at Berlin, New Hampshire, on February 29, 1964.

BOSTON and MAINE RAILROAD
GOOD IN COACHES ONLY
STATION STAMPED ON BACK To
BERLIN, N. H.
Good for One Passage in direction first presented within **ONE YEAR** in addition to date stamped. Subject to tariff regulations.
BC 4644 LC PASS'R TRAFFIC MGR.
38132

BOSTON and MAINE RAILROAD
GOOD IN COACHES ONLY
BOSTON, Mass. (B) To
WHITEFIELD, N. H.
Good for One Passage in direction first presented within **ONE YEAR** in addition to date stamped. Subject to tariff regulations.
BC 20835 LC GEN'L PASS'R AGENT
494

Above: Train 372 with RDC-3 6306 and an RDC-1 is about to depart for Wells River where it will meet up with train 32 from Montreal for the joint run to White River Junction and Boston. Donald G. Hills photo from August 1959.

Below: The local mail, train 431 to Berlin, is arriving in Gorham at 11:07 a.m. on July 11, 1956, behind GP-7 1557. The man emerging from the light blue station wagon is here to take the mail to the post office. Stanley W. Cook photo.

Above: E-7 3806 is "pretty as a pin" this summer day in 1953. She's at Littleton & Bethlehem station to help celebrate the 100th anniversary of railroading in America. The presence of the streamlined coach proves that at least occasionally these cars wandered off the Portland Division. Dana D. Goodwin photo/courtesy of the Boston & Maine Railroad Historical Society.

Right: The North Wind is a few moments from its departure from Bretton Woods-Fabian, New Hampshire for White River Junction, Springfield and New York at 12:10 p.m., July 11, 1956. Visible behind B&M road switcher 1559 are a New Haven parlor-baggage combine and a B&M "American Flyer" coach. This would be the train's last summer of operation; luckily, Stanley W. Cook was there to record the action.

On The River's Spine   197

A WEEKEND IN THE CONNECTICUT RIVER VALLEY

There are days in our lives that we will never forget... The wind stirred the moist, wooded air and created bobbing, silvery whitecaps out on the water. The buds were greening in the hills, and I could sense the thread of their bursting full leaves overnight. Puffy, white clouds blew across the crystal sky, dancing like playful lambs. This was one of the days when you are glad you're alive!

Don Ball, Jr.
America's Railroads

In April, 1963, my friends Lincoln Soule and Bob Meckley, and I, three avid 17 year-old B&M fans suffering pangs of spring fever, dreamed up a neat little three-day trip for Memorial Day weekend: we would take the 12:30 p.m. train, No. 31, from Boston to White River Junction, bicycles in tow, and pedal south by the Connecticut River line as far as Bellows Falls and North Walpole. There we would ride the Monadnock, Steamtown & Northern Railroad over the Cheshire Branch as far as the train went, then continue home on the bikes.

Our trip idea was partly the result of the urge to get out of the house and roam, but more specifically, all was not well with our train watching at home. I was bound by the limits imposed on bicycles, and while I have related the camping trip near Andover with Lincoln and his family, from where we made photo trips to Lawrence and Wilmington Junction, most of our train watching was done around Salem. That meant Budd Cars, which we thought lacked variety and color (how beautiful and clean they were in retrospect), the evening visit by the Talgo Train at a time of day when the light was too poor to get good photo results except in summer, and local freight service.

I longed for an E or F unit diesel, which I had seen only occasionally elsewhere and thought very beautiful, but none ever appeared. Even the GP9 "Bluebirds," which would have provided welcome color relief, were rare indeed.

We also knew that the days of the B&M's few remaining long-distance passenger trains were numbered. Each subsequent timetable seemed a little smaller. Even George Hill, the B&M's veteran P.R. director, was resigned to it. "What can you do," he moaned, "when we have an average of three passengers to Portland every day?" Marblehead, where we lived, had lost all its trains in 1959, and now even the tracks were gone. It was all so sad.

So, Saturday of Memorial Day weekend, a truly gorgeous New England spring day, Lincoln's Mom took us, our bikes, and a box of sandwiches in the old family station wagon into North Station. In our frequent visits to the station to watch trains we had discovered the private alley off Causeway Street to the east of the

On this southbound Ambassador, the five pieces of equipment are in five different paint schemes, very typical for this train—F-3 4228 in the McGinnis blue and white (with an ugly nose patch at that), GP in maroon and gold, RPO in Canadian National green, black, and gold, coach in CN's newer scheme of white and black, and finally a New Haven streamlined coach with a vermilion window stripe. Donald S. Robinson made this interesting photograph in the Massachusetts hills near Mt. Herman on June 6, 1966.

station. By driving in there we were able to get quite close to the train. To my surprise, there were *two* Budd Cars. From all I had heard about declining patronage, reportedly this and the afternoon train to Portland carried only single Budds. Our train, which would travel through to Montreal, had a 6200 series unit in front, so there was a baggage section where we put the bikes. The crew was wonderfully helpful; they were very friendly about helping to get the bikes aboard.

I sat with Lincoln and Bob for most of the trip south of Concord, New Hampshire, eating sandwiches, because there wasn't much of interest to photograph (How differently I would do it today!) Once through Concord, though, I rode alternately on the rear platform and in the baggage room where the crew left the door open so I could photograph, and the sights were indeed bracing. The extraordinary green brilliance of the scenery on the New Hampshire mainline bloomed before us. I suppose my limited budget explains why I have so few pictures of the trip, but I am thankful for those I did take. Though we sensed that this one daily passenger train from Boston to White River Junction might be in trouble for the future, it never crossed our minds that train service altogether might one day be a memory on this line. Let us hope that this glorious piece of railroad has not seen its last train.

Our train never seemed to go very fast. Rather, we just ambled along at a comfortable speed, always respectable and deliberate. The beauty of the land was exhilarating. Looking over my slides from the trip, I am impressed with how alive the scenery was, with magnificent colors everywhere. During the last half hour of the three and a quarter hour trip, the train began skirting the glistening sapphire waters of Mascoma Lake. With the sun darting in and out of puffy white clouds it was a stunning afternoon.

Two B&M GP-18s— "Bluebirds"— were on the turntable at the Westboro Roundhouse, and just ahead were two Canadian Pacific diesels. The sight made my adrenalin rush; I had never actually seen any of these maroon and gray diesels in this distinctive and distinguished paint scheme. Obviously I had come to the right place.

Since we had arrived at the end of Centralized Traffic Control (CTC), we stopped at the bridge before crossing the river, while our conductor walked across the tracks to the phone box by the signal mast and called

the Connecticut River dispatcher at Greenfield for clearance to enter White River Junction.

Our arrival at White River Junction, just after train 32 from Montreal via the Canadian Pacific, was out of sequence from the published timetable; next in line was the southbound Ambassador arriving over the Central Vermont line behind B&M 4226 A&B, wearing the first (and abortive) McGinnis attempt to combine B with M. Lord, what a terrible design! Fortunately, this was the only engine to receive this scheme. And yet, the other try, the now familiar standard logo was magically right, at least for me (As a kid, I practically worshipped B&M blue. That logo and its noble blue hue imparted a wonderfully sharp image to the railroad). The two-car consist carried a heavy weight Canadian National RPO and smooth sided coach, both resplendent in black, CN green, and dulux gold piping, another regal paint scheme.

Within a few minutes, the northbound *Ambassador*

Left: *The view from our train, somewhere on the New Hampshire mainline north of Concord.*

Right: *Our train is stopped in Westboro, New Hampshire, and the conductor has called ahead for permission to cross the bridge into the White River Junction Depot.*

Center: *There is a surge of passengers getting on and off the northbound Ambassador for Montreal. It carried a Canadian National RPO and two New Haven day coaches.*

Below: *F-2 A&B 4226—with its bizarre, one-of-a-kind paint scheme—leads the southbound Ambassador for New York with a CN RPO and coach. Four photos, RWJ.*

arrived behind B&M 4228 A&B, with another CN RPO, but this time carrying two New Haven streamline coaches striped in vermillion (Mrs. Lucile McGinnis, who selected this color, certainly had a flair for the dramatic.) Even as the passengers scurried about, changing trains, the locomotives pulled away, then backed around the train to the south. Business was brisk with lots of passengers; probably their numbers were swelled because of Memorial Day.

A new engine was coupling on the head end of the northbound *Ambassador*, and the sight of the train from the front was electrifying: a sparklingly clean Central Vermont GP-7 in shiny black, red, and white, with that elegant, simple CV noodle emblazoned on the side in white. The southbound Candian Pacific train to Boston was another pair of Budd Cars led by RDC 6211.

Here, for the record, is a summary of the published timetable for these trains (all times are p.m.):

No	Arr	From	Via	Dpt	For
32	3:45	Montreal	CP, BM	4:15	Boston
76	3:45	Montreal	CN, BM, NH	4:15	New York
31	3:50	Boston	BM, CP	4:10	Montreal
75	4:00	New York	NH, BM, CN	4:15	Montreal

We knew we had a long way to go before the Steamtown departure at one o'clock the following after-

noon, so we jumped on the bikes and headed south. Claremont Junction was our destination for the first night, 22 miles down river. Within a very few miles we were lucky to catch a glimpse of a northbound freight far off, crossing the river on a trestle near Windsor, Vermont, in the midst of a rolling green landscape.

We were enormously excited by the day so far. It had been thrilling and envigorating, full of new sights and bright colors, clear air, trains and adventure. It became more quiet and relaxed as we pedaled on for the next three hours, enjoying the simple sights. Rural New Hampshire and Vermont are very special, different from anything else in America (I really only learned this much later) and their subtle beauties are unforgettable. Only the sight of many "for-sale" signs on the little farm houses disturbed the placid impression. Young as we were we knew this hinted at a changing way of life.

At the end of that three hours hunger came on rather sharply. As the light began to fade we found a little country store on a quiet back road where we bought some food for supper. It was so peaceful and quiet, even compared to Marblehead, it seemed as if we had gone back in time to the 1920s. The packed dirt in front of the store, the creaky screen door, the dim streetlight just coming on with the dusk, the sounds of the crickets—it all seemed so far away from our world. We just sat on the bikes for a while, talking about the day and all the

Left: *Central Vermont road switcher 4925 is the new power for the northbound Ambassador. Inexplicably, the southbound train has backed its equipment up to the rear of the northbound.*

Above: *B&M freight JS-2 comes to a halt at Claremont Junction while a crew member makes a telephone call. On the point are three Alco RS-3s with 1514 in the lead.*

Right: *Claremont & Concord No. 17, a 44-tonner, switches tank cars at Claremont Junction. Three photos, RWJ.*

things we had seen. Then a gentle calm came over us and we didn't talk for several minutes; we just relaxed into the solitude of this quiet place. Eventually some energy returned, and after a few more minutes on the bikes we came to the Claremont Junction depot. The building had a big "for sale" sign, and I snapped a picture of the three bikes in front of it. Not too far away, we found a spot to camp. We pitched the tent, cooked some fish, and went to sleep.

Twice in the middle of the night we awoke to the plaintive sounds of diesel horns as the overnight *Montrealer* and *Washingtonian* thundered through the valley.

We awoke in the morning to some of the dampest air I had ever experienced, typical, I learned later, of what it is to be near a river like the Connecticut in the early morning. The fog was so thick I was sure the day was ruined.

Fog or no, we got dressed and made pancakes over the little fire, packing up quickly when we heard a faint train whistle coming down the valley. We got to the depot just in time and I was determined to make the single shot I would take "count" (I was low on color film). The fog had lifted quickly and the early morning light shone brightly on three pretty red B&M Alco RS-3s, which slowed helpfully as they approached. Not, as I imagined, to accommodate my camera, but for a yellow shirted trainman who jumped from the train to use the railroad telephone. This was JS-2, the morning freight from White River Junction to Springfield.

As the freight moved on to the south, a little red 44-tonner from the Claremont and Concord Railroad buzzed in the background demanding attention. I got a nice shot of it hustling a couple of tank cars. There was a time

Monadnock, Steamtown & Northern's No. 15 is nearing the hour of its mid-afternoon run down the Cheshire Branch in May 1963. Richard W. Symmes photo.

The Founder of Steamtown, F. Nelson Blount, is at the throttle of No. 15. RWJ photo.

when passengers from New York would disembark here and take a local train on the Claremont Branch for Lake Sunapee. The automobile has given us enormous freedom of travel, but it surely has taken away the charm and style of a tragically brief era.

We began the next 17 mile ride. As the last drops of morning dew evaporated and the sun climbed higher in the sky we found ourselves enveloped in another blue and gold day. An hour or so after starting out we came to

a hilltop from which we could see a vast expanse of river valley. It was as if the whole world were before us, and we three were the only ones lucky enough to be here at this wonderful time and place. Riding down the steep hill into the valley, we felt that tremendous rush of wind that only a cyclist experiences when the bike goes faster than anyone could ever pedal.

We duly arrived in North Walpole, New Hampshire, where Steamtown was located, just across the river from Bellows Falls. We poked around the exhibits, and I remember seeing the venerable old B&M dining car "Mountaineer" which had once carried Franklin Delano Roosevelt. It was named "Maine" then and got its new name after June, 1947 when it was rebuilt into a Diner-Lounge. It was not open to the public and we could only peer in through the dusty glass, but it was truly my favorite of the things to see. I loved the grand and rich look of such older B&M equipment. This same car was briefly on display a few years earlier at Pleasure Island on Route 128 in Wakefield.

After a little lunch, it was train time again, and we loaded the bikes into the combine, the rearmost of the four car train. All the cars were wooden coaches painted a bright chrome yellow, and each carried the colorful Steamtown emblem on the center side panel. The engine was 2-8-0 No. 15, ex Rahway Valley. We had a great time enjoying this steam train. I hadn't been on one (except at Edaville) since 1955 when I rode a morning commuter train from Marblehead into Boston with my Dad.

Our Steamtown trip lasted perhaps an hour as we casually meandered into the quiet, sunny countryside, some 15 miles on the Cheshire Branch, a slight uphill grade as we climbed away from the river. Along the route we passed people here and there who always waved, no matter what they were doing, and this made Lincoln, Bob, and me feel very important as we stood in the open baggage door of the combine. At the end of the trip the engine was run around the train in preparation for returning, in reverse, back to North Walpole. I took a picture of the engineer, F. Nelson Blount himself, the creator of Steamtown. We all spoke with him briefly; he was very nice to us. Then, with the tender in front and its headlight shining, this little country train of the Monadnock, Steamtown & Northern chuffed off into the baking afternoon sun.

After the train returned north, and we headed home over the base ridges of Mt. Monadnock, we didn't see, let alone ride, any other trains. The rest of the day's biking was wearying for me, though Lincoln and Bob thrived on it, and the remainder of the trip is a blur. The last color photo I took on that Steamtown train, somewhere near Westmoreland on the Cheshire branch, was a shot of our youngish conductor staring out the back vestibule, contemplating the passing of the land. My Dad always loved this picture, which he called "the last conductor."

How right he was.

Endnotes

1. Not nine cars as has often been reported. For details about the wreck, see *Interstate Commerce Commission Ex Parte No. 200, Accidents at Swampscott and Revere, Mass., Decided May 16, 1956.*

2. The B&M Employee timetables in the 1960s listed a location named "Wilson," 31.25 miles north of Boston. Named for Frank Wilson, the location marked the end of double track about one third mile south of Gloucester depot. It was a way of honoring him for his long career on the B&M.

3. The term "Winchester tower" is a misnomer. It was a square, one-story brick structure at street level. It survived the mid-1950s grade separation project which resulted in its being well below track level. The author was there on several occasions when train directors ran up the steep embankment to hand off orders to a train.

4. Two other grade crossings were eliminated in an earlier phase of the project.

5. Ray Tenney was often referred to by B&M employees as "McGinnis's hatchet man," and was a man of whom they steered clear.

6. The *Wildcat* is a three-mile connecting track linking the New Hampshire mainline with the Portland Division Western Route. It was built as the Andover & Wilmington Railroad in 1836, and soon became the first route of the Boston & Maine.

7. H. Bentley Crouch compiled a list of local freights operating in the Spring of 1942, in "March 26, 1942, Twenty-Four Hours Recalled," *B&M Bulletin*, Volume VIII, No. 2. Freight Train Symbol books for 1954 and 1962 are in the author's collection.

8. "The Gloucester Branch," by Ed Brown, *B&M Bulletin*, Volume XIII, No. 2.

9. "Not On the Timecard," by Dana D. Goodwin and H. Arnold Wilder, *B&M Bulletin*, Volume X, No. 1.

10. "Where Did The Freight Go?", by Dwight A. Smith, *B&M Bulletin*, Volume XV, No. 2.

11. "Memories of the Lexington Branch," by George Dimond, *B&M Bulletin*, Volume XIII, No. 1.

12. "When the Railroad Came to Medford," by Walter E. Lenk, *B&M Bulletin*, Volume XII, No. 2.

13. "A One Man, Two Day, Two State, Five Railroad Fan Trip," by Dwight A. Smith, *B&M Bulletin*, Volume XI, No. 4.

14. "Woodsville: A White Mountain Terminal," by H. Arnold Wilder, *B&M Bulletin*, Volume IV, No. 4.

Bibliography

Ball, Don, Jr. *America's Railroads: The Second Generation*. New York: W. W. Norton, 1980.

Boston & Maine Railroad. Public Timetables, 1946-1970.

_____ . Employee Timetables, 1933-1965.

_____ . Freight Train Symbol Books, 1953, 1960-64.

Baker, George Pierce. *The Formation of the New England Rail Systems*. Cambridge, Mass: Harvard University Press, 1937.

Brown Ed. "The Gloucester Branch." *Boston & Maine Bulletin* 13,2: 20-27.

Byron, Carl R. "The Hoosac Tunnel: The Mohawk Trail by Rail." *B&M Bulletin* 3,1: 5-14.

Crouch, H. Bentley. *The Central Mass*. Reading, Mass: Boston & Maine Railroad Historical Society, 1975.

Crouch, H. Bentley. "March 26, 1942: Twenty Four Hours Recalled." *B&M Bulletin* 8,2: 7-18.

Crouch, H. Bentley. "The Pemi" *B&M Bulletin* 5,2: 20-29.

Crouch, H. Bentley. "The 'Phantom' Division." *B&M Bulletin* 8,4: 5-25.

Crouch, H. Bentley, and Frye, Harry A. "WN&P—All Those Branches." *B&M Bulletin* 9,2: 21-31.

Daggett, Kenneth M. "Portland, Saco & Portsmouth R.R." *B&M Bulletin* 9,4: 13-18

Dimond, George. "Memories of The Lexington Branch." *B&M Bulletin* 13,1: 6-9.

Fisher, Ralph E. *Vanishing Markers*. Brattleboro, Vt: The Stephen Greene Press, 1976.

Frye, Harry A. *Minuteman Steam: Boston & Maine Steam Locomotives, 1911-1958*. Littleton, Mass: Boston & Maine Railroad Historical Society, Inc., 1982.

Garland, Joseph E. *Boston's Gold Coast: The North Shore 1890-1929*. Boston: Little Brown, 1981.

Goodwin, Dana D. and Wilder, H. Arnold. "Not On The Timecard." *B&M Bulletin* 10,1: 12-31.

Holbrook, Stewart H. "The Great Rail Wreck at Revere." *American Heritage* 8,3: 26-29.

Humphrey, Thomas J., and Clark, Norton D. *Boston's Commuter Rail: The First 150 Years*. Cambridge, Mass: Boston Street Railway Association, Inc. 1995.

Hutchinson, Leroy C. "Streamlined Train No. 6000 Scheduling History." *B&M Bulletin* 11,3: 29-33.

Kennedy, Charles J. "Railroads in Essex County A Century Ago." *B&M Bulletin* 5,3: 22-29.

Lenk, Walter E. "When the Railroad Came to Medford." *B&M Bulletin* 12,2: 5-8.

Longhi, J. Norman, ed. "The Saugus Branch." *B&M Bulletin* 8,3: 21-28

Neal, R. M., *High Green and the Bark Peelers*. New York: Duell, Sloan and Pearce, 1950.

Smith, Dwight A. "A One Man, Two Day, Two State, Five Railroad Fan Trip." *B&M Bulletin* 11,4: 7-11.

Smith, Dwight A. "Where Did The Freight Go?" *B&M Bulletin* 15,2: 26-32.

Symmes, Richard W., and Hornsby, E. Robert. "Elmwood Junction, New Hampshire." *B&M Bulletin* 4,1: 10-19.

Tobey, Raymond E. "The Portsmouth, Great Falls & Conway R.R." *B&M Bulletin* 12,4: 4-16.

Tobey, Raymond E. "Tracks Along The Connecticut." *B&M Bulletin* 14,4: 6-25.

Valentine, Donald B. Jr. "The Forest Line." *B&M Bulletin* 17,1: 6-11.

Whitney, Scott J. "From Ashuelot to Ashes." *B&M Bulletin* 14,1:28-31 and 14,2: 32-35.

Wilder, H. Arnold. "Passengers to the White Mountains." *B&M Bulletin* 5,4: 5-18.

Wilder, H. Arnold. "The Stony Brook Branch." *B&M Bulletin* 8,3: 5-12.

Wilder, H. Arnold. "Woodsville: A White Mountain Terminal." *B&M Bulletin* 4,4: 5-18.

Index

Errata and Comments

We are indebted to numerous readers who wrote with corrections and comments about the first printing of the book, especially to Donald Robinson whose knowledge and expertise have helped to clarify the record. We have included here anything we thought could be of interest, although there were a few reader musings too long for inclusion. There are a few differences of opinion, in which case we simply include opposing views without comment.

The page number shown refers to where you will find the photo or text in question. Sometimes the actual caption is on the opposite page, but the header words, such as "Below," "Far right," etc., are *always* the same as printed in the book.

p. 9, photo: This must have been taken no later than early 1953, since that's when the Expressway rampwork started. From Carl Byron. See also p. 52 photo note.

p. 11, paragraph 4: Alden Dreyer writes: "Strange, but what bothers me most was George Drury's mention of the operating ratio in 1955 of 76.51 percent.. Why couldn't George have picked a more typical year when the operating ratio was well over 100? 1955 was the only good year the B&M had between 1928 and liquidation. Sure, it had an even lower operating ratio in 1932 (the last year of the dividend) but business was off a full third from three years prior.

"The B&M showed earnings of over $3 million in 1955—just a little more than it lost in 1954. But the railroad was in desperate straits and it knew it. For the first time B&M management seriously questioned its survival. Hiring and maintenance were severely cut and that, combined with exceptionally mild weather and wonderful carloadings, made 1955 a good year."

p. 25, paragraph 6: Alden Dreyer writes: "Electrically controlled switches and signals were either 'hot wired' or code. 'Hot' wiring works just like the wiring in your home or automobile. Code had nothing to do with a simple computer as there was no mathematical function nor information processing . . . A code machine was a simple mechanical device that functions very much like a rotary dial telephone . . . " (Donald Robinson suggests "direct wire" rather than "hot wire.")

p. 25, paragraph 6: Regarding the parentheses at the end of the paragraph, Donald Robinson writes "Also red indicator lights were used within interlockings; yellow or white elsewhere."

p. 28, paragraph 2, line 4: Alden Dreyer writes: "Lynn Tower did not have 'hundreds' of mechanical levers as you want to imagine. It was a large tower but forty levers was standard for most towers as that was the number one man could handle without reaching total exhaustion."

p. 29, photo: According to Don LeJeune, the engineer is A. J. Sullivan, the fireman Jerry Quinn, and, on the platform, left to right, are Arthur O'Donnell, Frankie Morin, and Sammy Whitmore.

p. 43, 1st paragraph: Carl Byron writes: "A Budd Car weighed between 52 and 65 tons depending upon configuration (RDC-1, -2, -3, -9), well over the 45-ton limit of the Brotherhood Agreement. Thus,

negotiation of the 'Union Concession' was necessary to allow one man operation." The author originally planned to use this version for the book, but changed it when two sources proposed the scenario which was printed.

p. 43, 1st paragraph: A "call on" was, and is, a steady bottom yellow, through which an engineer may proceed, not exceeding 15 mph, being prepared to stop short of any train or obstruction. When flashing it is a "slow approach," i.e., proceed at 15 mph through turnout(s), prepared to stop at next signal. From Donald Robinson.

p. 44, photo: This type of crossing signal was generally known as a "wig-wag" (from the swinging arm), although the manufacturer's name was "Automatic Flagman." Of the many which once protected B&M highway crossings only one remains [as of 1991] in service at Richardson's Crossing on the Hillsboro Branch between Milford and Wilton and that rarely sees a train.

The highway and railroad drawbridges at Beverly are not and never were operated by the same person, although the two men obviously do communicate with each other in order to coordinate the openings. From Donald Robinson.

p. 51, Below: According to Brian L. Jennison and Dave Engman, the green coach is recently purchased from the Reading Railroad, still in its original color, but with B&M lettering.

p. 52, Lower left: Note that the trainshed roofs are coming down in preparation for placing the ramp footings. From Carl Byron, Dave Engman.

p. 53, Above: Donald Robinson notes that this train was not a likely candidate for the Central Mass because of the P-2 Pacific. Although they were technically permitted on the branch, he never saw one there. Perhaps it is a train for Fitchburg or Lowell. Also from Dave Engman.

p. 55, text: Dave Engman notes that the Boston Engine Terminal is in Somerville.

p. 63, right column, line 8: "site" not "sight"

p. 65, Above left: Dave Engman suggests this locomotive is actually 2726 or 2728 since 2720 had an Elesco feedwater heater.

p. 70, Right: same as p. 63.

p. 96: According to David Q. Olsen (via John F. Kane), the *East Wind* is shown at Millbrook Street near the B&M yard (the first yard to be removed).

p. 97, paragraph 3: Alden Dreyer writes: "Your grouping of the Lowell Jct. to Worcester line was curious. The route *may* have been double tracked in 1929, but you implied that the entire route received CTC in 1929 when actually only 13 miles of it did. . ." According to Donald Robinson, Worcester to Ayer was double-tracked in stages in the 1880s by the original owner, the Worcester & Nashua.

p. 97, Below: The train is *arriving* from Peterboro and is *unloading* mail and express. From several readers, including the photographer.

The Peterboro local was affectionately known as "Mike Downey's Train." Mike was the conductor, and for years the railroad kept this old coach in service because his arthritic legs could manage its four vestibule steps but not the newer ones with three. From Donald Robinson.

p. 97, Bottom: Two readers suggested that this was the Lowell rather than the Peterboro train, because of the presence of the steel coach. However, the Lowell train left very early in the morning, and the shadows here indicate that it is already quite late. It is winter time, with snow on the ground, so probably the Lowell train left before daylight. Also, photographer Stephen Payne confirms that this is the Peterboro train.

p. 102, last word: "lesser" not "lessor"

p. 106, Above: Donald Robinson states this to be Crescent Lake, with Lake Wentworth a half mile to the left.

p. 110-111 map: Missing are track segments from Tilton to Franklin Falls, Contoocook to Emerson (South Henniker), and Lakeport to Lily Pond. From Donald Robinson.

p. 112, Below: The location is *North* Chelmsford. From Donald Robinson, Dave Engman.

p. 118, Below (also p. 121, Below): Donald Robinson writes: "Note the flag stop signal in front of the station. Of the 'hundreds' I saw I know of only one still standing and that is not used. Supposedly whether the white was toward or away from the track determined for which direction it was displayed, although I cannot remember ever seeing any instructions posted for the public. Many had chains which permitted the hanging of lanterns at night."

p. 119, line 4: "Winchester *and* Main Street"

p. 119, Top: train *310* not *302*. From Donald Hills.

p. 122, Below: Dave Engman notes that, although there are eight coaches, they are ex-PRR P54s, shorter than most coaches.

p. 126, Left: The location is actually Pinardville, a section of Manchester, NH. West Manchester was the closest station to the south, Grasmere Junction to the north.

p. 127, Center: Dave Engman writes: "Steam generators were in the short hood. *These* humps were for head-end lighting for certain groups of commuter coaches. The new (1930s) B&M 1200 series used HEP lighting and several steamers had a large turbo generator on top of the tender behind the coal bunker for this purpose." Also from Brian L. Jennison.

p. 135, paragraph 2: "met passengers at *Plymouth*" (not Concord). From David J. Smith.

p. 136: Donald Robinson writes: "When I first remember the EB&L it had two active locomotives—a Shay and a 2-4-2T—both #5! It must have driven the ICC bonkers."

p. 137, Above: Though the train is in the town of Ashland, the nearest station is Bridgewater, just to the right of the picture. From Donald Robinson.

p. 140, paragraph 5: Alden Dreyer writes: ". . . only about 25% of the traffic on the Fitch went into the Boston area to feed the *Camel* and other locals, not the 60% you mentioned."

p. 140-141, map: "Clinton Junction" not "Sterling Junction." The Hollis Branch is missing. From Donald Robinson.

p. 143, Right: Dave Engman suggests the pusher is on the Central Mass rather than the Fitchburg (they were parallel here). Donald Robinson confirms this; it is an ammunitions extra for the East Sudbury dump during World War II.

p. 143, Below right: Route *20* not *128*. The construction site is on the place of the former Stony Brook station. From the late Norton D. Clark (the photo was taken *from* the Route 128 bridge). Donald Robinson writes: "I remember the grade crossing which was eliminated by the bridge shown. During construction, traffic used the road, the remnant of which shows beside the front of the train. Its crossing was torn out when the bridge opened (this was the first Route 20)."

p. 144, Above left: The train is *eastbound* not *westbound*. From several readers.

p. 144, Below left: Donald Robinson writes: "5507 is a Cheshire Branch number and therefore is headed for Bellows Falls, Vt., not Troy, N.Y. However, it will stop at Troy, N.H., and this caused endless headaches. It was a rare day that we did not have at least one passenger on the wrong train out of Fitchburg." Dave Engman writes that most of these head-end cars are D&H milk cars. Donald Robinson counters that these look like B&M 1600s in Bellows Falls Creamery service, or possibly Rutland or CV, and that D&H cars served in N.Y.

p. 150, Above left: The train is *westbound* not *eastbound*. From several readers.

p. 154, Above: Donald Robinson writes: "Although it was at the other end of the station, the picture of Troy reminds me of Gaynor's, a popular 'watering stop' for railroad men. At the time New York state law only said that a bar must be closed four hours out of 24; it didn't say which four. Gaynor's had two separately operated bars connected by a lockable door. One bar was closed 2:00 a.m.-6:00 a.m. and the other 6:00 a.m.-10:00 a.m.; the rest of the time the door was open and so were both bars."

p. 157, paragraph 3: Donald Robinson writes: "Gleason Junction was not a diamond since the Central Mass bridged the Marlboro Branch (and also the Maynard & Hudson trolley). A quarter-mile ramp track connected the two. The Central Mass end was Gleason Junction which was for a time a train order office. The Marlboro Branch end was called CM Junction. The Central Mass for a brief period carried a Boston-Harrisburg express. Freights rarely went beyond Berlin after the abandonment of Oakdale-Rutland."

p. 159, Top: This photo was actually taken by the late Norton D. Clark, though the author did review a virtual twin view by Donald Robinson.

p. 159, Bottom: Donald Robinson writes: "The 'elbow' gate arms allowed the tips to drop to clear the overhead wires when the gate was raised. A wire attached to the base pulled it out when the gate was lowered." Locomotive 1455 resided at Edaville for many years after its retirement. It was moved to Hyannis in November 1993 where it was cleaned and painted for display by the Cape Cod Railroad. Restoration efforts are still hoped for.

p. 163, Below: *Near* Kendall Green would be more accurate, since the actual station is on the Fitchburg. From Dave Engman. Near *Weston* would be more accurate still, according to Donald Robinson.

p. 165, Near left: Dave Engman wonders if this could be 1496 on the excursion of April 25, 1948. Donald Robinson confirms that magnification of the transparency appears to favor 1496.

p. 167, line 8: Donald Robinson writes "Steamtown was on the C&C the year before it went to Keene and used a different locomotive. The trek from Pleasure Island to North Walpole was a never-to-be-forgotten 12-hour trip which took three 16-hour days. Getting the engines out of Pleasure Island to the B&M Topsfield Branch was ever after known as 'The Battle of Snyder's Swamp.' There also was a year operating out of North Walpole to Westmoreland before going on the Rutland."

p. 169, Below: The train consists of 22 over-dimension brewing tanks for the then-abuilding Budweiser Brewery at Merrimack, N.H. From Donald Robinson. Also Carl Byron.

p. 170, paragraph 2: Track between Peterboro and Elmwood, and between Hillsboro and Emerson was abandoned as a result of the flood of March 1936, not the hurricane of September 1938. From Donald Robinson.

p. 170, paragraph 3: Donald Robinson writes "New Haven President F. C. Dumaine, Jr., leased the RS-3 to the B&M for $1 per day for the Peterboro train so that he could dismantle the steam servicing facilities at the NH's South Worcester enginehouse where the B&M engine was kept."

p. 176, photo: Alden Dreyer writes "The gorgeous photo of Jack Falvey entering Bellows Falls with the icicles masks the story about the most expensive wreck in B&M history that necessitated this detour." Carl Byron adds that the detour was in effect for about 10 days.

p. 178-179, map: Donald Robinson writes: "Technically the B&M used the CV between Norwottuck (South Amherst) and Canal Junction (east of Belchertown) and the B&A between Forest Lake (east of Bondsville) and Creamery (three miles west of Wheelwright). Ware, being the largest town on the branch, should be shown in the B&A section. Originally the B&M had its own track in both of these sections. Use of the CV and B&A started in the early 1930s. Isolated sections of B&M remained in Ware and Belchertown to serve customers.

East Northfield, an important junction with a 24-hour train order office, is missing from the main line. Dole Junction is also missing at the junction of the Ashuelot Branch. CV track should be shown in Vermont between East Northfield and Brattleboro; both it and Windsor to White River Junction should be identified as 'CV track dispatched by B&M.' When I started dispatching, orders for extra trains specified 'Via Vernon' or 'Via Dole Jct.' Later the CV was designated the 'southward track' and the B&M the 'northward track'."

"Bretton Woods (Fabyan)-Whitefield (at, not north of) and Waumbek Junction-Coos Junction should be shown as "Maine Central Track." The B&M once had its own routes Whitefield Junction-Coos Junction and Wing Road-Fabyan-Base Station but found trackage rights cheaper in later years. It did retain a wye and small yard at Fabyan as long as it operated the summer passenger service. Before the advent of Guilford, the B&M purchased Waumbek Jct.-Coos Jct. from the Maine

Central when the MC abandoned Quebec Jct.-Beecher Falls."

p. 180, Above left: According to Dave Engman, this is not 3620, which had an Elesco feedwater heater, and which he thinks was scrapped before the war. Donald Robinson: "I won't argue; my records were not the best in those years."

p. 180, Below left: The location is *South* Deerfield.

p. 181, Below right: Donald Robinson writes "This train is 712 not 72. It and its northbound counterpart 717 had CV crews between White River Junction and East Northfield, with CV power White River Junction-Springfield and a mixture of B&M-CV-NH equipment. I saw Pacifics only a few times (and once with a Consolidation), but from the late '40's to the end of steam the power was usually a Mountain (with an air horn—ugh!)."

p. 183, Above: Donald Robinson writes: "Technically this location is West Claremont, and the station was just north of the bridge. The south abutment of the old bridge is visible under the locomotive." An old pier is visible under the B&M "American Flyer" coach.

p. 187, Left: This is perhaps CP train 904. From Dave Engman. Donald Robinson: "More likely 908, as shadows show it is late afternoon."

p. 195, Far right, bottom: The location of the trestle is Gorham not Berlin. From Donald Robinson.

p. 197, Right: Donald Robinson writes: "Station name is Bretton Woods-Fabyan (not Fabian). The original Bretton Woods was about a mile east, and while it existed, *this* station was called just plain Fabyan. The MEC Bretton Woods station was a platform behind and part of a summer hotel while the B&M station was a platform across the road from the front of the hotel. Neither had a separate building although the B&M's did have benches and an awning. Service was seasonal, and I know nothing about ticket sales."

p. 198: Donald Robinson writes: "As a point of interest the CN RPO was lettered 'U. S. Mail.' They had several such for international trains although, to the best of my knowledge, no mail was sorted in Canada. International RPO routes were designated between: Boston-Alburgh, New York-Alburgh via Rutland; and Boston-St. Albans, New York-St. Albans via CV (there may have been others)."

p. 199, caption: The correct spelling is *Mt. Hermon*. From Alden Dreyer.

p. 202, paragraph 2, line 4: Carl Byron writes that the locomotive is a GP-9.

Pine Tree Press publishes Errata Sheets for all its books. Please send corrections to P. O. Box 39484, Los Angeles, CA 90039. If you would like a copy of any Errata Sheet, please send a self-addressed stamped envelope to the above address and state the title you wish.